Why Your Website
Doesn't Work

Why Your Website
Doesn't Work

How to get your message
right, focus your website,
and stop losing business

Chris Davidson

ISBN (1st Edition):   978-1-7392307-0-8 (Paperback)
                        978-1-7392307-1-5 (Hardback)
                        978-1-7392307-2-2 (Ebook)

Cover by Scott Graham
Typesetting by Megan Sheer

Why Your Website Doesn't Work by Chris Davidson (1st Edition)

Website Toolkit
Content & Links

You've bought much more than a book: you've bought a complete website improvement toolkit that includes an online website assessment and a content improvement tool. Both the assessment and content tool have been field-tested on client projects, some of which are presented as case studies in the pages that follow.

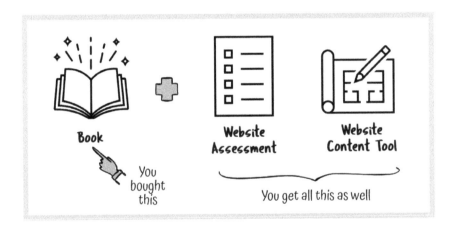

Book

You bought this

Website Assessment

Website Content Tool

You get all this as well

Website Effectiveness Assessment (WEA)

https://chrisdavidson.co.uk/wea

The WEA is an open access tool that measures your website's effectiveness. The customized report will help you prioritize your use of the book's content to improve your website. Having your personal report available as you read the book will be helpful, so I recommend you get it delivered to your inbox before diving into the details.

Product-Client Alignment Matrix (P-CAM)

https://chrisdavidson.co.uk/p-cam

P-CAM helps you create impactful written content that generates more business. A step-by-step user guide forms part of this book. Once downloaded, P-CAM is yours to keep and use as many times as you wish.

Before You Start

There's a good chance you're here because you've stumbled into a rarely discussed truth: *making effective business websites is hard*. This fact is at odds with many marketing messages suppliers would have you believe. Adverts suggest you can 'build a professional-looking site with this new online system' or promise you can 'quickly create a beautiful site with no tech support'. Many such claims artfully sidestep the increasing number of complex challenges facing business owners grappling to create an economically effective online presence. I'm here to give you an objective, balanced view—and the tools to deal with reality.

There's a world of difference between a blog that chronicles your hiking holiday and your company website. The former does not need to reach a wide audience to fulfil its function. The latter, meanwhile, needs to reach as many of your target audience as possible. To do so, it needs to perform flawlessly on every device. It needs to rank high on a Google search. Of course, visitors should be so excited and enthused by your content that they willingly hand over their contact details to stay in touch with your latest developments. And while we're at it, wouldn't it be great to sell some online courses to boot? Achieving all this is really hard. Don't beat yourself up if you're having a tough time.

This book is primarily for service-oriented businesses in the SME (Small to Medium size Enterprises) sector. Service businesses have a hard job focusing their message, as the benefits of what they sell are frequently less tangible than those of consumer products. If you run a product-oriented business, you will still find this book useful, just note that I've chosen mostly service-based examples and case studies to illustrate my points and recommendations.

The answer to having an effective business website doesn't lie in additional flashy technology (whatever the adverts claim). The answer lies in your head—and I'm going to help you get it out.

To illustrate what I mean, here's a hypothetical scenario: Tom and Mary are excellent amateur photographers, keen to improve their art and win more competitions. Tom is convinced he needs a new camera, even though he doesn't use the full capability of the one he has. Mary has similar equipment and believes she needs to focus on improving her own skills, so she can get more from the kit she already owns. If this book were about photography, Mary would buy it (and Tom wouldn't).

Regardless of what camera you have, acquiring the skills to capture beautiful, impactful photographs takes dedication and years of practice. Better light meters or more lenses might help, but there aren't any shortcuts for the dedication and practice required to become a skilled photographer. The same is true for building websites. As you work your way through the book, I'll show you where you are on your journey and suggest what you ought to do next. I'll give you a new framework and tools to help you. Your job is to dedicate the necessary time and practice and put to use what you learn. You can learn a lot from reading a book, but you'll realize the benefit by applying the work to your website.

Websites are easy. Effective, highly engaging business websites are hard. Having one will make your life better and your business more successful. I've been in IT for more than forty years—before the term 'information technology' even existed. I was part-author of the IBM Consulting Group methodology and later established the consulting services division for a specialist IT supplier within the aviation sector. I set up my consulting company over twenty years ago and have helped hundreds of clients improve their service-oriented businesses (see the case studies in Part G for examples). Since 2017, my colleagues and I have conducted an annual worldwide survey of thousands of business websites (mostly in the SME services sector). I've presented the results at industry conferences on both sides of the Atlantic and Pacific. I know the challenges and I've created a successful team that helps clients overcome them.

I've got your back. Ready?

Contents

PART F: CLIENT ALIGNMENT (WEF TIER 5)

PART G: CASE STUDIES

WTF to OMG:
Start Here

Nobody ever steps in the same river twice,
for it's not the same river and they are not the same person.

—Heraclitus

Written 2,500 years ago, the Greek philosopher's wisdom perfectly reflects the state of IT in the third decade of the 21st century. Company owners revisit the technology river, seeking a better website. Since their previous visit, the river has become a torrent, and some lose their footing. This book will help you keep yours.

If you're struggling to sell your services through a website that empties your bank account instead of filling your calendar, this book is for you. Your marketing approach may be more *outdated* than *wrong* and that may be creating a weak target focus (WTF) that's the root cause of your problems. The internet era fuelled a dramatic shift in marketing over a relatively short time, leaving many businesses playing catch-up. Broadcast techniques dominated 20th century marketing. The 21st century ushered in a much stronger focus on niche marketing. This book will help you understand where you're going astray and help you get back on track.

In the twenty-plus years I've been running my IT consultancy, I've come across hundreds of companies that have struggled to clarify what they are selling and to whom. They've poured a ton of money and shedloads of effort into building websites for little return. Their lack of clarity and inability to engage the right audience explains that poor return.

It stands to reason that companies that cannot clearly explain what they sell will also struggle to find the right audience. Once they have clarity, engaging the right audience becomes much easier. This book will help you achieve clarity and will also help you engage the right audience. Equipped with this information, you'll get better results when you come to spread your message wider.

What's at Your Fingertips?

If you read this book, use the tools provided, and complete the exercises discussed, you will achieve three outcomes. First, you'll produce better written content for your website. Second, you'll be able to better interpret what IT people tell you. Third, you'll develop a more finely tuned bullshit detector. This is invaluable given that IT is a rapidly changing and largely unregulated market, with many people trying to sell you stuff you don't need.

Why Your Website Doesn't Work will help you focus your website on the needs of your clients. It will also help you identify and correct common technical issues that impact website search engine rankings. You'll find this useful if you maintain your own website or manage external help.

If you're a copywriter, designer, or agency, you'll also find this book useful—not for your own needs—but to help your clients gain clarity on what they want before engaging you. This will help reduce project friction, improve efficiency, and make for happier clients.

This isn't a book about website technology. I've kept geek-speak to a minimum. Any remaining is there because, as a business owner, you ought to know it.

This is a book about you, your website, and your business. The book promises to tell you *'How to get your message right, focus your website, and stop losing business'*. I'll be clear about when I'm stating fact or offering opinion. In 2017, I launched the Worldwide Digital Footprint Survey. This annual review of thousands of websites has helped me understand the challenges facing the SME sector and focus this book on areas that will deliver the most benefit to business owners.

The additional software tools—the WEA and P-CAM—are part of the book and integral to your reader experience. They will help you unlock the full value of the combined book/toolkit approach.

Website or Funnel?

A website is a Swiss Army Knife, and a funnel is a surgeon's scalpel. A website does many things reasonably well. A funnel does one thing exceptionally well. A scalpel is a special knife, and a funnel is a special website. This book applies to both websites and funnels. I use the term 'website' (or 'site') to refer to both websites and funnels. I highlight any content that's uniquely applicable to funnels.

An example website: Websites typically deliver information on a range of topics. A menu system connects multiple information pages and makes the website more manageable. Users are free to roam across the site however they like. Websites frequently contain blogs. These are a special classification of webpage. Blogs store their pages in order of publication date, although it's possible to further organize the content using categories and tags.

An example funnel: In contrast to the freedom to roam provided by websites, funnels take visitors on a narrow, focused path. Users either follow the path or leave the site. There's no menu system that gives users the ability to roam (apart from links to legally required pages, such as terms and conditions). Including emails as part of a complete marketing funnel is a common option, particularly where the aim of the funnel is lead generation.

How to Use this Book

This book and the associated tools are the distillation of a core idea I've been working on for approximately six years. You can use the materials if you already have a website, or if you're just at the idea stage. I've presented the content in the best sequence for readers who already have websites. If that's you, then read the book as it's presented.

The following order will suit you better if you have a bright idea but still have to build your website.

- Read Parts A and B. This will set the scene and introduce you to the new Website Engagement Framework.

- Then skip to Part F and read about 'moving the goalposts'.

- Now work your way backwards, reading Part E next. This will help you create content for the site you are going to build.

- Part D will give you ideas for engaging visitors once your new site is online.

- Part C will help you better manage the building of your site, so make sure you've read it before you engage additional help.

You'll find case studies in Part G, towards the back of the book. These provide real-world examples from those who have used the tools and approaches you'll shortly learn about.

This is the first book of the Website Wisdom collection. At the end, you'll find more about book two. Right now though, it's time to deal with Website Challenges.

Part A

Website Challenges

1.

Why Your Website Is In Crisis and Why It's Not Your Fault

Many business websites are in crisis. I first realized this several years ago after getting feedback from my clients who came to me confused and panicked about how ineffective their current sites seemed to be. The clamour grew, and in 2017 I ran a survey to seek more significant data. Since then I've conducted an annual worldwide survey of business websites[1], focusing on the SME services sector. Although there are a couple of positive trends, overall the results do not paint a pretty picture. Too few business owners can detail how their websites contribute to their business. Many seem to have one just 'to keep up with the Joneses'.

As technologies have developed, websites have grown in technical capacity. Some business owners have recognized this and moved their websites from being 'an online shop front' to more central, revenue generating roles. However, there's a worrying number of business owners who still seem to maintain an arm's length relationship with their websites (and IT in general). It reminds me of when I started working in IT. In those days it was called 'data processing', and IBM had an entire division called 'DPD', the Data Processing Division. Regardless of the label, this nascent industry

---

1   The Worldwide Digital Footprint Survey is designed and conducted by my company, Active Presence Limited.

Figure 1-1: The
IT pendulum in
the early 1980s,
when computing
was complex,
eye-wateringly
expensive, and the
preserve of experts.

was complex, eye-wateringly expensive, and the preserve of young engineers who spoke a language nobody understood. It lived in a back room somewhere and ran the monthly accounts (Figure 1-1). IBM introduced the PC in 1981 and it took off in the early 1990s with the dawn of the internet. Microsoft and Apple were in the vanguard of companies that democratized computing by creating software that average Joes and Janes could use. One no longer needed an engineering degree to tap into the power and efficiency of computing technology. The internet connected these computers to one another and other services, and that connectivity stimulated explosive software growth. New technology companies blossomed, and productivity headed skywards (Figure 1-2).

The high rate of technology development ushered in ever-bigger challenges, as illustrated by the struggle suppliers had in complying with Rule Number 1 of website design: deliver a good experience to all visitors. The smaller size of the early 21st century internet

Easy
Cheap
Available to all

1990s

IT in the 1990s

Figure 1-2: The IT pendulum in 1990 as Microsoft and Apple (among others) democratized computing. The internet was about to change the world.

made it easier for websites to deliver comparable experiences to all users. In April 2002 there were 558 million internet users[2] and approximately half a dozen different internet browsers[3], including the newly released Firefox browser.

However, developments came thick and fast. Steve Jobs proudly unveiled the iPhone in 2007. In 2008, Android responded with their offer and Google launched its Chrome browser. Jobs was back on stage again in 2010, showing off the iPad.

By mid-2012, the number of internet users had multiplied fivefold, reaching approximately 2.5 billion. Browser choice had doubled, and users now wanted internet access while on the move, via handheld devices nobody had imagined a few years previously. All this within a decade. Developers had to work their socks off to 'deliver a good experience to all users'.

2   https://www.internetworldstats.com/emarketing.htm
3   https://en.wikipedia.org/wiki/Timeline_of_web_browsers

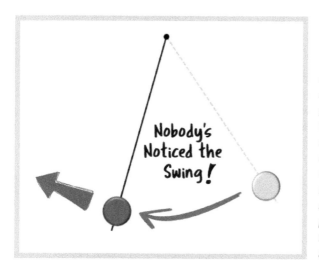

Figure 1-3: Although IT is more powerful than it was decades ago, it's also becoming as complex as it was then. Too few business owners seem to have prepared themselves for the challenges ahead.

As is always the case, new technology triggered more change. Software suppliers started creating applications that moved websites from the back office to customer-facing roles. For example, increasingly complex ecommerce systems, online diary scheduling, and—as driven home by the COVID-19 pandemic— video conferencing. The pendulum that swung from 'complex' (in the 1980s) through to 'easy' (in the 1990s) is now swinging back towards 'complex' (Figure 1-3). The worrying point? Many SME business owners don't seem to have noticed, which brings us full circle to the crisis I mentioned at the start of this chapter.

No wonder some business owners feel overwhelmed. We expected IT would carry on being easy, cheap, and available to all. The tide has changed. IT is reverting to being complex, expensive, and crucially, the preserve of experts.

Running your business effectively entails working out how to thrive in this new environment. You need to know enough about the technology landscape to ask the right questions, interpret the answers, and hire the right people to help. The next chapter will help you do this.

NUTSHELL NOTE #1

Many business owners haven't kept pace with the development of website technologies. Websites can play a more significant role than many business owners realize, but they are becoming harder to implement.

2.

The Lies Website Owners Tell Themselves and Whom to Ask for Help

As the IT pendulum swings back towards 1980s-era complexity, I've noticed that many website owners cling to practices that aren't going to serve them through the third decade of the 21st century and beyond. Here are common misconceptions I come across.

"I have someone who does all this for me"

No, you don't. Someone may have told you that—and that person may have genuinely believed what they were saying. But website technologies are far too complex nowadays for one person to possess all the skills at the required level to deploy them effectively. It's no longer possible for one person to design your website; finesse the background code; run an effective SEO campaign; and design, launch, and manage your online ads (for example). Each area requires expert skills.

If website production started life as a four-piece garage band, it's grown into a full-scale symphony orchestra. This chapter will help you manage the additional musicians who've recently joined the ensemble.

"I could do the whole thing myself"

Not a chance. One casualty of the latest swing of the pendulum is the plucky amateur hoping to knock up an all-singing all-dancing website for their business on a Saturday afternoon. The range of expertise needed exceeds the capacity of any single person. Even if you had the skills once upon a time, you no longer have enough to do a good job in today's world.

You're the expert at what you do, and it's your expertise that generates your income. You can't direct your effort elsewhere without losing money. If building websites is not your business, you shouldn't be doing it.

"I use social media for marketing; websites are outdated"

Where would you prefer your loved ones live: a home you own or rented accommodation with a lease heavily biased in the landlord's favour? If you wouldn't select the latter for your loved ones, then you shouldn't pick it for your business either.

Social-media platforms and third-party suppliers such as Google and Microsoft can change the rules at a moment's notice to suit themselves. Feel free to play in their backyard, but have a space you can call your own.

"My work is so complex; I have to explain it to my clients one-on-one"

The COVID-19 pandemic taught us all to find alternative ways of interacting with our clients. Those who didn't suffered. Some are no longer in business. Your clients are online. If you're not there with them, your competitors may be courting their attention.

"I use my website as a brochure/shop window"

I've heard this phrase used in slightly different ways, but the root cause is the same: the website owner doesn't have enough time or understanding of current technology to consider a more central role for their website. Lack of time or other more pressing business issues may have kept the website at the bottom of the to-do list. In other cases, previous website upgrades have not worked as expected. With everyone feeling sore about a failed project, the easiest decision is to leave the site as a 'brochure/shop window'.

I feel for all these website owners. During our conversations they realize their website has strayed off course. They're like the lost traveller asking for directions and being told, "If you want to get there, I wouldn't start from here".

Two Additional Jobs to Avoid

Another outcome of the return swing of the IT pendulum is that website owners are encountering people whose skill sets and titles they may not understand (Figure 2-1).

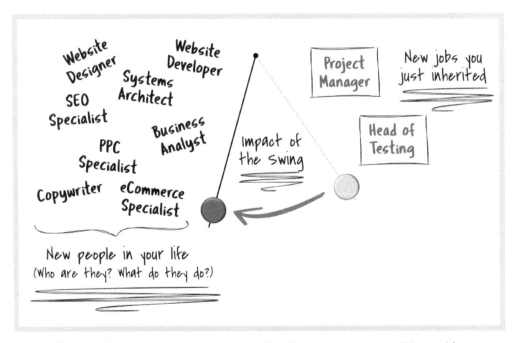

Figure 2-1: The expanding reach and complexity of websites has increased the need for specialists. Many small businesses lack the ability to assemble and manage such teams.

Along with these new people, Figure 2-1 also illustrates two new roles to which website owners frequently find themselves unknowingly appointed: project manager and head of testing.

Testing: A worrying trend I've come across in smaller website projects is suppliers making their clients responsible for all testing. Frequently, this seems to happen unconsciously. Suppliers omit testing from their proposals, and by default, clients accept the role—even though they lack the skills to perform it well. Testing is a huge topic, and an IT profession in its own right. You ought to be testing *some* of the supplier's work, but not *all* of it.

Well-managed IT projects have many testing milestones. You don't need to know about all of them, but you should know about the systems test and the customer acceptance test (CAT). These two tests are major milestones and test different but complementary aspects of your new website.

The supplier should execute the systems test. Its purpose is to show that the website the supplier has built (the system) complies with the client's specification. When the systems test is complete, the client conducts the customer acceptance test. Here's a simple example:

During the systems test, the supplier verifies that the lead magnet sign-up form collects data correctly and sends the required emails at the right time. They also check the online shop to verify that it's possible to buy all the products offered and that any discount codes work correctly.

Too many times, I've seen this sort of testing shoved onto the client's desk, by way of a casual email, for example, "Hi Jim, we've completed the online store – have a look and let me know what you think." If problems later surface and the client complains, the supplier responds with, "Well, you tested it and were happy with it then."

This is all very different from, "Hi Jim, we've completed the online store and we're reasonably confident it works the way you want. The summer and winter discount codes work, and the

T-shirts are showing as available in 4 different sizes and 5 colours. Please have a look and let us know if we've overlooked something."

Once the systems test is complete, the client acceptance test can take place. The focus of the CAT ought to be on aspects of the site that rightly belong with the client. They will want to verify the company address and phone number, check that the company logo is the latest version, that product names are capitalized according to the style guide, that all staff names are up to date and connect to the correct LinkedIn profiles, etc.

During a recent conversation with a young website designer, I asked about his approach to testing. He replied, "I email the site link to the client and ask them to click on all the buttons and tell me if anything is wrong."

You can see how this approach is neither fish nor fowl. It's an ill-defined mélange of part systems test and part acceptance test, with no plan and no proper record of results. You should take responsibility for the CAT and give your supplier advance notice of what you'll be testing. Insist on the supplier conducting a systems test. Ask to see the test plan and documented evidence of the results. This may increase the project's timescale and cost, but I believe it's time and money well spent. Your job is to run your business, not be a part-time, untrained IT tester.

Project management: Many smaller businesses run 'slim and thin' as regards project management. It's assumed to be a general management skill that any competent manager (frequently the business owner) can perform. Managing IT projects requires different skills than managing a building site, for example.

Modern approaches to IT projects favour build cycles with multiple quick releases. In my experience, few non-IT experienced managers cope well in this environment; they are frequently overloaded with too many other tasks. Once deadlines start slipping, projects unravel quickly.

Unless IT-savvy folk have been involved right from the start, scope creep is inevitable. Non-IT business managers frequently lack awareness regarding the level of detailed planning needed for IT projects.

While writing this book, I declined to bid for three website projects. My no-bid decisions had nothing to do with the book writing workload. All three clients wanted a fixed price bid, but none could provide sufficient detail for us to size their project accurately. They weren't being obdurate, they simply lacked an understanding as to what was required. My explanation declining the opportunities went along these lines:

'You're asking a builder to quote for a substantial building project based on a relatively simple textural description. For example, 'I'd like you to build me a detached 4 bedroom house, with 2 bathrooms and a separate double garage'. Although that description seems reasonable to you, without the architect's plans, there is no way I can provide an accurate bid. I do not know what foundations are required, what sort of heating is required, whether you envisage air conditioning, what standard of glazing or rendering is required, etc. If I were to quote a price and the project were to start, I can guarantee the absence of any plans would lead to you making many additional requests. Costs would escalate and deadlines would fly by like feathers in the wind.'

I meet some business owners who seem unable to divorce their *business processes* from their *website*. The result is that website designers end up taking decisions that really belong with the business owner. The way your business works belongs to you, not to any website designer.

This confusion commonly occurs the first time a business implements ecommerce. For example, let's imagine a business implementing ecommerce assumes their new online store will handle volume discounts the same way its offline business does when processing national, in-country orders. Suppose volume discounts for the in-country orders are based on the total order value (including postage and packing).

What happens now that international orders can be placed online, from almost anywhere? International orders have much higher shipping costs than their national, in-country equivalents. In percentage terms, the value of product in an international order is smaller than in a national order—the difference being the shipping charges.

However, the process dictates that volume discounts are set by the total order value (not the value of the product shipped). The result is that international orders might attract volume discounts that would not be offered to national customers. While this is a win for customers, the company would be losing revenue by discounting orders that would not have been discounted by the offline business.

Clearly, the volume discount rule needs changing to account for the much wider range of shipping charges resulting from the company's move into international sales. This is a *business* issue, not a *website* issue.

Of course, it's unlikely any business would calculate volume discounts in such a simplistic way, but it's a good illustration of the need to check existing business processes against new developments, to ensure the business remains well served. Many business processes develop organically and simply become the de facto way of getting stuff done. Own your processes and establish clear demarcation lines between *business* and *website*.

It's time to look at the new roles (to the left of the pendulum in Figure 2-1) and review whom you need to hire and when.

Typical Roles You Ought to Understand

Increasing complexity makes teamwork essential for IT projects, as no one person can do it all. To understand what a business does— how it captures data, manipulates it, and then uses it to serve its customers' needs—is a complex undertaking.

Here's an introduction to the roles typically needed in modern website projects. You won't need all these people all the time, but you will need all these skills some of the time. Depending on their skill level and experience, you may come across some specialists who combine roles and go by a different title.

Marketing strategist

You want this person to be around for the long-term. The marketing strategist sits at the interface of marketing and IT, and sets expectations for the business owner and the IT team.

You should trust your marketing strategist the same way you trust your accountant. You share everything that's going on so they develop a complete view of your business, inside out and back to front. Just like your accountant, they won't be in your office every day, but they add immense value when they are.

I've come across many business owners who mistakenly believe they can do this themselves. While it's tempting to believe that nobody could know more than you about what you do or the market you serve, this misses several points:

1. The marketing strategist will have experience with other web-design projects. This helps them create realistic deadlines and track progress. In this context, they're bringing project management skills to the party.

2. They act as a decision maker and communications channel. They know when to decide on the owner's behalf and when to call in the owner for higher-level decisions.

3. Their knowledge of your business makes them the ideal person to keep on board after the current work is completed. Websites are like puppies; they need constant attention, training (optimization), and feeding (content).

Business analyst

The role of the business analyst (BA) is as old as IT itself, so it's worth knowing what they do. Business analysts are experts in understanding what a business does with the data it has. It's easy to appreciate how a business analyst is going to be way more important to an international bank than the corner grocery store. That said, many smaller businesses are venturing into ecommerce, which automatically produces more complex data flows. For example:

- Credit card transactions need to be securely processed

- Order confirmation emails need to be generated and sent

- Order-shipped emails also need to be generated and sent, perhaps including order-tracking links

- Order history needs to be updated and stored

- Perhaps marketing campaigns need to be triggered, based on order history

- Perhaps discounts need to be offered, based on previous order history

The relatively simple thought of, 'Let's sell our stuff online' quickly snowballs into a complex project, capable of generating way more data than the (offline) business has handled up to this point.

Smaller businesses won't have enough work for a dedicated BA. However, understanding the role can help you address BA activities for your own project. Typically, an ecommerce specialist could cover the BA data flows for modest ecommerce ventures. You could also reasonably expect the marketing strategist to contribute.

Systems architect

When I joined the nascent IT sector in my early twenties, the role of 'architect' didn't exist[4]. The internet triggered a rapid expansion of new technologies, platforms, programming languages, etc. As projects became more complex, both in scope and in the number of subsystems, a need arose for someone to define the various technology components projects would use. That person is the systems architect: the person who recommends what IT components should be used to achieve the project's business goals.

As with business analysts, smaller businesses won't have enough work to need a full-time systems architect. However, understanding the role can help you make key decisions consciously, rather than by default. For example, you might employ an ecommerce specialist who recommends using Shopify, simply because they know the platform, as opposed to it being the best ecommerce solution for your needs.

Systems architecture decisions have long-lasting consequences. Once you're committed to a particular ecommerce system, for example, changing it is complex and expensive. More than likely, you can combine the systems architecture skills required for smaller projects with another role. Ideally, look for people with long IT careers, who have worked on diverse projects, preferably in the same sector and for similarly sized businesses.

Designers (of various sorts)

As the IT sector has matured, the term 'designer' has developed. It's a much-misused label, so it's worthwhile to clarify its various uses.

---

4   The IT sector's attempt to use the word 'architect' caused a bit of a faff, especially in the UK, where the title 'architect' is a professionally protected term. Eventually the title 'systems architect' was accepted by all involved.

Graphic designers are specialists at using images to communicate concepts. They know about fonts, colours, layout, typography, etc. For many, the bedrock of their early career was advertising (especially print advertising, if they are an older designer). You'll also find many have worked in marketing, communications, or branding.

Website designer is an informal label that has arisen through common usage. The arrival of high-quality content management systems (Squarespace, for example) gave graphic designers new openings—they could now create good looking websites for grateful clients. This market has been successful for many years, but cracks are starting to appear. The advertising background of many graphic designers leaves them ill-equipped to deal with the current swing of the IT pendulum (back towards 1980s-complexity).

As websites have increased in complexity, it made sense to break down design into more specialist areas. The Wikipedia entry for 'web design' is a useful starting point for understanding what website designers do. It refers to 'web design' as the "many different skills and disciplines in the production and maintenance of websites". The same article talks about graphic design, **user interface (UI) design**, and **user experience (UX) design**. Within IT, these terms are well understood and used in preference to the general label of 'website designer'.

Outside the IT bubble, clients and suppliers alike use the term 'web designer' as a catchall term for several distinct functions within IT and website development. If you believe you need website design skills, it's worth questioning yourself in more detail, to see if you can arrive at a more specific set of requirements.

- **UI design focuses** on your website aesthetics. UI design is highly visual. For example, can people easily find the information they're looking for? Do they intuitively know what action to take?

- **UX design** focuses on how well your website works. UX designers concentrate on removing friction. They want to create a website that makes it easy for the user to achieve what the business owner wants. UX designers are skilled in research, testing, and validating alternative designs. (For this reason, some UX designers prefer the label UX specialist, as opposed to designer.)

So, if someone describes themselves as a 'website designer', what exactly do they do? Good question. Nowadays, anyone with good UI or UX credentials would call them out loud and proud. If someone describes themselves as a 'website designer', I'd interpret that as a 'Jack or Jill of all trades', with potentially greater strength in the visual (graphic design) side of website building. I would check their credentials and experience carefully, prior to engaging them. Ask them for examples of their work and get them to explain their contribution to you, rather than just send you images to look at, or links to click. For example, "I see you have [xyz company] website in your portfolio. Could you describe the design process and highlight your role within it? For example, did you design the page layouts based on templates created by an architect, or did you take responsibility for the website architecture? The same site has a client portal. Who was responsible for coding the registration system—was that you, or another developer?"

You get the idea. The term 'website designer' is a bit of a mess, especially at the smaller end of the market. Don't be afraid to dig deep, so you get a good picture of the individual's overall skills. I'll close this example by noting that if they had strong IT skills, they might prefer to call themselves a website developer—see next.

Website developer

Website developers work with code. They use programming languages and other technologies to make a website function as required by the design specification. They're not concerned with what it looks like, they're concerned with what it does. They work closely with UX specialists.

Other specialist roles

Beyond the foundation work of actually building your website, there are various specialists who can help you improve it. Their roles are more self-explanatory and easier to grasp.

The aim of Search Engine Optimization is to help your target audience discover your website. The **SEO specialist** improves your organic search engine ranking. They research the search terms used by your perfect clients and focus your website on responding with high quality content. They might also edit your site layout, to improve the response of search engines. The ultimate goal is to have your website appear on the first page of search results. Over two-thirds of all clicks go to the first five organic results[5] and fewer than 1% of Google searchers bother with results on the second page[6]. SEO used to be something that website owners could do themselves. However, the growth in the number of sites and their complexity has made SEO an expert domain, even though some basic concepts have remained (such as the importance of backlinks).

The natural companion to organic traffic is traffic you pay for (via advertising of some form). Pay per click (PPC) advertising is the most common form, in which you pay when users click on your advert (and get directed to your website). Advertising is a complex area. A lot of testing and tuning is required to get adverts performing well, i.e. attracting traffic that converts well for a reasonable outlay. **PPC specialists** can help you focus on the important variables for your situation.

---

5   https://www.zerolimitweb.com/organic-vs-ppc-2021-ctr-results-best-practices/
6   https://backlinko.com/google-ctr-stats

This is a book about websites and not PPC, so I'm going to limit myself to some fundamental points and a few recommendations. There are many excellent books and online resources about both SEO and PPC. I read books about SEO and PPC to help me better select and manage specialists, not to do either job myself.

Some ways a PPC specialist can help you: the major PPC platforms (e.g. Facebook, LinkedIn, Google, Amazon) have their own business objectives, none of which involve being parsimonious with your advertising budget. If you show them your bank account, they'll delight in emptying it. PPC advertising works by running an auction between advertisers wanting to bid for the same advertising slot. The winner isn't necessarily the person who bids the most, but the person whose advert is most likely to succeed. Specialists will help tune your adverts, so you can get more clicks for fewer dollars.

The job of the PPC specialist is to use your budget wisely to generate high volumes of the right traffic and deliver it to where you tell them. If the traffic fails to convert, that could be the fault of where the traffic lands and not of the advertising. There's little point in a PPC specialist working hard to produce perfect leads if those leads end up on a home page full of non-specific, wishy-washy copy. PPC works best when it's used to generate traffic for a highly specific niche offer. The page at which that traffic arrives should focus on the needs of the PPC-generated audience. For this reason, PPC-generated traffic is typically directed to highly focused funnels (and not websites offering general information).

Ecommerce is another area that has developed rapidly and now benefits from specialist attention. Ecommerce shares a similar development history to SEO and PPC: early shopping carts had limited functionality and could be configured by any competent designer. Nowadays, **Ecommerce specialists** work with systems (such as Shopify) that are so rich in function they can replace an entire website, as opposed to being an adjunct to an existing one. In the WordPress world you can find dedicated ecommerce plugins (such as WooCommerce) and there are plenty of WordPress experts who make a good living just focusing their efforts on WooCommerce and leaving the 'ordinary website setup' to others. If you're going to implement ecommerce, start by drawing all the data flows you can think of, which might include marketing emails, for example. You'll be amazed at how extensive and complex such a drawing becomes. (See also the earlier section on Business Analysts.)

If you also decide to implement some PPC advertising to send more traffic to your new ecommerce site, you can quickly see the need for specialist support.

Copywriters

Copywriters are the unsung champions that underpin all successful websites, funnels, and landing pages. Based on years of preparing winning proposals, many business owners believe they can write persuasive sales copy. However, writing for the web differs from writing offline documents: there is much less space available to get the job done, so it requires direct, efficient writing. It uses specific techniques to capture and hold attention, and lead towards an outcome. This difference makes it worth hiring a pro. You'll find them worth their weight in gold.

To create an effective, engaging website, you need to:

- Have the right people in the right place at the right time

- Be able to explain what you want them to do

Part B will help you do this.

NUTSHELL NOTE #2

The complexity of modern website technologies means you need a team to realize the benefits for your business. Getting the right help early on saves time and money in the long run. The tighter the initial specification, the better the end result. IT projects need specific management skills, and website owners shouldn't assume their general business management skills will suffice.

Part B

Website Effectiveness Framework & Assessment

3.

The Website Effectiveness Framework

Suppose we're part of a small island community. We live our lives happily and comfortably enough from the natural resources of the surrounding sea and land. Basic industry has established itself and we're a reasonably prosperous community.

Some of the more adventurous merchants want to expand by trading with other island communities whose islands lie further out to sea than we've ventured up to now. Planning meetings throw up some immediate and obvious needs:

- The boats needed to reach the other islands have to be more seaworthy than the small inshore fishing craft our shipwrights are used to building.

- The new boats also need to be equipped with navigation systems to help them find the off-lying islands.

- Local merchants need to supply products that (a) can survive the journey, (b) are useful to the occupants of the other islands, and (c) can fit in the cargo holds of the new boats.

We build some larger craft, make some voyages, and start trading. Some early success helps lift everyone's spirits. However, along the way, we also encounter some problems:

- Some products don't survive the journey and arrive in a non-saleable state. Being of no further use, the crews jettison them overboard.

- Some merchants cut corners and don't insure their cargos. They cannot recover from having their goods jettisoned and eventually cease trading.

- Some products survive the journey well, but the inhabitants of the off-lying islands aren't interested in them.

- Tragedy strikes and several boats are lost at sea. Some were not as seaworthy as at first thought. Some were overloaded and should never have set sail.

The problems and loss of life take their toll on our community. At a public meeting, we vote to take action to improve safety, preserve life, and improve overseas trade. The merchants create the 'Island Trading Safety Board'. Its job is to come up with minimum standards to which the inter-island trading craft must adhere.

Local merchants pool their funds to support several 'market exploration' voyages. They use the best of the remaining boats and load them with small cargos of sample merchandise. Being lightly laden, the boats sail faster. The merchants hope to complete their exploratory voyages quickly and learn more about the interests of our neighbours—what type and quality of goods they find appealing, etc.

It's easy to overlay this story on your website.

You Need a 'Seaworthy' Website

There is little point in briefing a copywriter to produce beautiful sales copy if your website is technically unsound. When it comes to your website, Google is judge and jury; they are the Island Trading

Safety Board. Google issues clear technical guidelines you should follow. Where Google goes, others follow. All major search engines discriminate against sites that don't meet minimum technical standards, no matter how useful the content might be.

You Need to Find the Right Market

The market exploration voyages depended on the boat crew's navigation abilities and equipment. No matter how well you know your target market, you still need the capability to find potential clients and engage with them.

You Need Sample Products

Just as the merchants (eventually) took sample products on their voyages, you need to offer your audience a trial product or service so they can determine if they want to buy from you. In online businesses, these trials are frequently trial subscriptions, free assessments, or other lead magnets that allow potential clients to sample your services at minimal risk.

You Need the Right Product

The merchants didn't fully understand the needs of the inhabitants of the off-lying islands, so they wasted time, money, and energy trying to sell products based on their best guess. The better you know your client's needs and can meet them, the better off you and your client will be.

Although all these elements are interconnected, a natural order is self-evident. There's little point in equipping an unseaworthy ship with excellent navigation systems and filling the hold with valuable cargo. So too for your website; there's little point in spending a small fortune on copywriters and designers if your site is going to be ranked poorly by Google. The allegory survives further scrutiny. Filling the hold of a seaworthy ship with valuable cargo is pointless if you can't navigate safely to the destined market. Little point then in having a technically superb website with cracking products if your clients can't find it, or you're unknown to them. Figure 3-1 summarizes this interdependency.

While this natural order suggests a sensible sequence of work, you don't need to follow it slavishly if you have resources to run and manage multiple work streams. For example, the shipwrights could build more seaworthy boats at the same time as the merchants are building higher-quality products more capable of surviving their time in the hold.

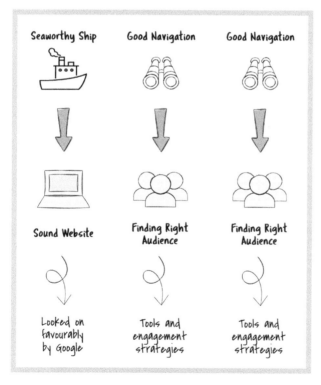

Figure 3-1: An illustration of the interdependency between technology and marketing, when improving website performance.

The Work to Fix a Poorly Performing Website

The work needed to fix a poorly performing website divides into three categories:

- **Technicalities** relating to how Google views and ranks the site (along with the other search engines). Thankfully, many of these issues can be resolved with a one-time fix.

- Issues relating to how the site engages the target **market** and attracts visitors. Unlike 'once only' technical work, market related work is continuous and relentless, needing constant attention.

- Issues relating to your **products**[7] and how they satisfy the needs of the market.

If you want to improve the performance of an existing site, start by identifying and resolving outstanding technical issues. If you're starting from a blank canvas, start with your products and clients—you can address the website later.

It's possible to capture all this in a helpful framework that you can apply directly to your website, and this takes up the rest of Part B.

The Website Effectiveness Framework

The Website Effectiveness Framework (WEF) comprises five tiers. Figure 3-2 illustrates how they align with the three major categories highlighted in the previous section.

I developed these five tiers from working with clients, combined with the results from the annual Worldwide Digital Footprint

---

7   Unless explicitly stated otherwise, I use the word 'product' as a shortened form of 'product or service'.

Survey. Coming chapters give you the details of each tier, and access to an online tool to assess your website against the framework.

To start, here's an explanation of Figure 3-2, summarizing each tier, explaining how each relates to the challenges the islanders faced and the relevance to your website.

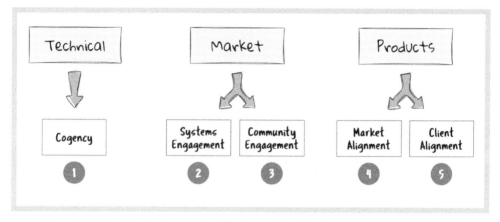

Figure 3-2: How the challenges faced by the trading islanders (technical, market, and products) map to the Website Effectiveness Framework.

1. Cogency

This is the most process driven tier. It measures the validity of your website's technical configuration. The aim is to ensure your website ranking isn't being held back for technical reasons. This tier is the foundation. It's equivalent to the islanders' basic requirement of having to build seaworthy craft. Without seaworthy craft, all their other efforts would amount to naught.

2. Systems Engagement

The two 'engagement' tiers are complementary. Both relate to discovery and engagement with your perfect clients. The systems engagement tier builds on the technical foundation established by the cogency tier. Systems engagement addresses how well your website attracts and communicates with visitors (via systems such as sign-up forms, online chat, call back, etc.).

3. Community Engagement

The second 'engagement' tier has more to do with you than with your website. Community engagement measures how well you're recognized as being a significant contributor to the community you serve. Evidence could be the number of people seeking your opinion on sector issues or asking you for help with their own challenges. People with high community engagement scores have a significant social media following.

During their voyages, some of the trading islanders might have created good relationships with people living on the off-lying islands. The trust that developed between the visiting merchants and the people living on the islands would increase the merchants' community engagement scores—they became trusted commercial partners.

4. Market Alignment

The two 'alignment' tiers focus on the products you deliver to solve your clients' problems. Your website will have a high market alignment score if it offers specific products that solve genuine problems your perfect clients find challenging. The tighter the fit between the market's needs and your products, the better your market alignment, and the greater your chance of selling more products.

Based on my work with clients, this seems to be a very challenging area for website owners. I've created a tool to help you produce much better website content. You'll find chapters dedicated to it later.

5. Client Alignment

A successful website would have high scores in all the first four tiers. Client alignment is optional, in that it's possible to have a successful business without paying much attention to it. If that's the case, what is client alignment and why bother with it?

Client alignment is for people who want to rewrite the rule book and introduce a new normal to the market they serve. It goes beyond just having an excellent set of products that serve your community well. A high client alignment score introduces a permanent step change in how (some aspect of) the market operates. This helps you carve out a unique niche in the market, which can help drive more business.

How the Website Effectiveness Framework Helps You

The framework gives you a vehicle for communicating with the different IT roles you read about in Part A. Figure 3-3 shows how common website problems map to the framework tiers.

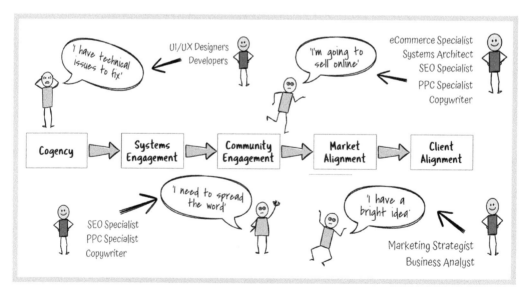

Figure 3-3: The IT skills needed to resolve common issues and how they map against the Website Effectiveness Framework. You need a team approach; no one person can do all this.

"I have technical issues to fix"

Technical issues belong to the cogency tier, and you'll need UI/UX designers and developers to help you resolve them.

"I need to spread the word"

To spread the word about your business, you need to find and engage your target market. Both the engagement tiers will be involved, and the important skills will be copywriting and traffic generation, whether by boosting organic traffic volumes or by purchasing traffic through advertising.

"I'm going to sell online"

I've already mentioned how complex ecommerce can become. You need someone to identify the best ecommerce platform for your needs. That could be a systems architect or ecommerce specialist. You'll need someone to map out the data flows and code the shop and checkout (ecommerce specialist). You'll need to drive traffic to the shop to get sales, and that could need SEO and/or PPC specialists, plus a copywriter.

"I have a bright idea"

Congratulations: you have an idea that will revolutionize your market. You'll need a marketing strategist to help you convert that into something you can sell. You'll probably need business analysis skills to make sure you're taking care of all the additional data the new system will generate.

To improve your own website, it would be helpful to know how it performs for each of the WEF tiers. The Website Effectiveness Assessment does this for you. The next chapter tells you how to access the assessment and interpret your results.

NUTSHELL NOTE #3

The Website Effectiveness Framework (WEF) gives business owners a structure for categorizing the common technical, marketing, and product-oriented challenges faced during website development. This helps save time and money by focusing effort where it's most needed.

4.

How to Interpret the Website Effectiveness Assessment

Website Effectiveness Assessment (WEA)

https://chrisdavidson.co.uk/wea

The Website Effectiveness Assessment positions your website within the Website Effectiveness Framework by awarding numerical scores for each tier. The scores help you decide where to focus your efforts.

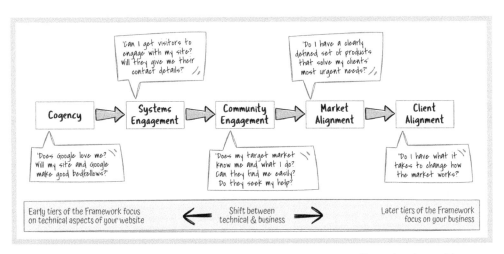

Figure 4-1: The focus of the Website Effectiveness Framework, illustrating how with each tier focus shifts from technical issues to business issues.

The IT sector is so unregulated and rapidly developing that it's easy to get carried away by the latest self-proclaimed guru or shiny new 'must have' piece of software. Figure 4-1 summarizes the focus of the framework.

Cogency

The focus of this first tier is the technical foundation of your website. Will the search engines love your site and promote your content?

Systems Engagement

Once you get visitors to your website, the site must provide value to help gain trust and develop a relationship.

Community Engagement

The more social proof you can provide, the easier it is to develop online relationships. Encouraging your followers on other platforms to visit your website and engage with your content also helps cement your website's relationship with the search engines.

Market Alignment

This tier addresses how you satisfy your clients' most urgent needs with a clearly defined set of products.

Client Alignment

The final tier becomes relevant if you have a unique idea that could create a permanent change in the way (part of) your target market works.

Progress through the first three tiers comes naturally enough. It makes sense to fix any technical issues (cogency) prior to promoting your site to your target market (community engagement). Likewise, it also makes sense to have some means of engaging visitors (systems engagement) prior to creating a tidal wave of traffic that would otherwise flow through your site like water off a duck's back.

As you progress through the tiers, the bar at the bottom of Figure 4-1 shows how the questions shift focus from technical to business issues.

If you haven't already done so, now is a great time to run the Website Effectiveness Assessment:

https://chrisdavidson.co.uk/wea

Interpreting Your Website Effectiveness Assessment

The assessment delivers a PDF report to your email inbox. There are six percentage scores in the report, the first being your site's overall effectiveness. The remaining five correspond to each of the five tiers. Figure 4-2 shows example scores for three imaginary businesses. Working through these will help you understand your own report. Look for outliers when you review your report, rather than focusing on the absolute numerical score for each tier. Do any scores stand out as being much higher/lower than the others?

Dog Grooming & Walking (DGW)

DGW's website has a low Cogency score (circa 30%). All other things being equal, Google will discriminate against DGW's site. We can't tell what the issues are by looking at the score in isolation. However, returning to the story about the islanders and their voyages, we can say the site is 'unseaworthy' in some way and it's likely that a modest investment would help the site compete on a more equal footing for search returns. DGW's failure to take care of the technical basics is hindering their success in other areas of the framework.

By contrast, DGW's score for Systems Engagement is much higher. Perhaps they offer online dog grooming tips to which

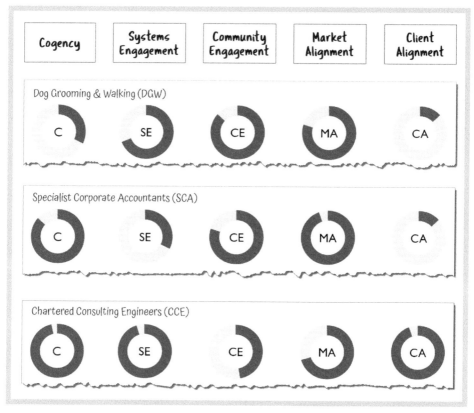

Figure 4-2: Three example businesses illustrating the Website Effectiveness Assessment.

visitors can subscribe? Good Systems Engagement is only worth the traffic you can send its way. The low Cogency score will decrease the volume of organic traffic that search engines send to the site.

DGW's high Community Engagement score is their ace card. Clearly, they position themselves well on the social media applications used by their dog-loving target market. Perhaps they offer dog-grooming tips via Facebook Live or post video snippets of their dog-walking activities on Tik Tok. This high Community Engagement score is probably responsible for driving a lot of traffic to the website, where it's dealt with by a reasonable Systems

Engagement configuration. DGW's reasonable website traffic and engagement could well be masking the low Cogency score. Their success at driving traffic through Community Engagement makes up for their impeded organic search performance.

The respectable Market Alignment score suggests the site contains clearly defined products specific to their target market. An example could be an online booking system for scheduling dog grooming and walking.

The corresponding low Client Alignment score tells us that DGW isn't doing anything new or groundbreaking in the world of dog grooming and training. Instead, they focus on providing the expected standard products and connecting with their target market through social media.

You can see how the report tells DGW where to look for quick wins: Cogency. DGW should check the technical setup of their site. Following that, a detailed review of how they engage visitors and present their products might lead them to additional improvements.

Specialist Corporate Accountants (SCA)

Now that you have some experience interpreting the individual doughnut charts, can you suggest where SCA should go looking for quick wins? If you said, "Systems Engagement", then you're bang on the money.

The high Market Alignment score suggests the SCA team has a well presented, comprehensive range of products. Their high Cogency score comes from having a technically sound and well organized website. The firm enjoys a respectable Community Engagement score, which could drive a reasonable volume of traffic to the website. However, what happens to that traffic when it arrives? The Systems Engagement score suggests the site might be leaking leads, with prospective clients leaving without engaging. How could SCA verify this?

Google Analytics would give SCA an idea of traffic volume and bounce rates[8]. If SCA also had access to visitor-journey analytics, they would get a clear view of:

- The source of their visitors. This would tell them how effective their Community Engagement is in driving traffic to the website.

- The route their visitors take through the website. How many of their visitors reach the all-important product pages (Market Alignment)? And where do they leave the site?

- The effectiveness of their existing engagement systems. There may be some quirk of design that's causing visitors to miss the opportunity of engaging with SCA.

Visitor-journey studies deliver great insight and are an important step in analyzing and tuning a website. (More on this in Chapter 6.)

Chartered Consulting Engineers (CCE)

A high Client Alignment score is rare, but it jumps out when scanning CCE's results. This immediately tells us that CCE has created something special that's capable of changing how their market operates.

The high scores for Cogency and Systems Engagement tell us that CCE has a technically proficient website capable of engaging visitors. Of the three example businesses, CCE has the lowest scores for Community Engagement and Market Alignment.

How can we make sense of these charts? What story are they telling? Perhaps CCE is a relatively new company and they're still

---

8   Bounce rate: the percentage of visitors leaving a site having only viewed one page. See Chapter 6 for an update on this metric.

building their social media presence. That would explain the lower Community Engagement score. Maybe they've invested shedloads of time and effort into their groundbreaking idea and they've yet to convert that into a full suite of products; that could explain the lower Market Alignment score. The high Systems Engagement score could suggest a desire to build an audience they can target when their products are complete.

In the real world, this would need verifying with the business owners; however, it's an example of how the Website Effectiveness Assessment can give you some useful background.

Your assessment report will suggest which tier of the framework would be the best starting point for you. Use the list below to access chapters on each tier directly or continue to read, tier-by-tier.

- Part C—Cogency (Tier 1)
- Part D—Systems & Community Engagement (Tiers 2&3)
- Part E—P-CAM User Guide (Tier 4)
- Part F—Client Alignment (Tier 5)

NUTSHELL NOTE #4

The Website Effectiveness Assessment (WEA) scores the effectiveness of your website against the five tiers of the Website Effectiveness Framework. The scores help you prioritize your website-development efforts.

Part C

Cogency
(WEF Tier 1)

5.

Fixing the Foundations

As part of the first COVID-19 national lockdown, the UK government suspended all building work and closed down the construction sector. The situation was grim: building sites lay empty and silent, as did all the companies making up the vast supply chain of the construction sector.

One smart building-materials supplier could see the way the wind was blowing[9]. To keep his business afloat, the owner laid off most of his staff, taking advantage of the government-backed staff-furlough scheme. He had previously invested in a capable website and believed strongly that technology was a driving force in his business. While the website's ecommerce capabilities weren't particularly well developed, the business had a good online stock database, including inventory levels, product descriptions, etc. Long-term investment in search engine optimization had resulted in the website getting lots of traffic and being well positioned in search engine returns. This company had the basics well organized.

Confident in his vision, the owner poured a shedload of money into the website, most of which was spent on improving the ecommerce capabilities. Remember, this was when his business was producing zero income, and nobody knew when the economy would reopen.

When construction work restarted, this building supplies company ran rings around its competitors. The company was soon generating 80% of its pre-COVID revenue with 20% of the staff. Nowadays,

9   A true story. The company is known to me but doesn't want to be named.

the shop at the front of the yard is like a morgue. Tradespeople don't bother visiting anymore; they order online, directly from building sites, using their mobile phones. The business—and the sector it serves—has reshaped itself in a profound way.

It's true that this business owner was smart enough to see the change coming and reposition his business to capitalize on the opportunity. However, it was his steady investment in technology over the years that gave him the edge over his competitors. His website had firm foundations and was already performing well, making it easier to add additional capability.

How about you?

If you have a low Cogency score, check the following points. Do this prior to investing truckloads of time and cash into SEO campaigns, copywriters, etc. Make sure your IT team has addressed these points:

- HTTPS

- Mobile experience

- Google's Core Web Vitals

- Optimized metadata

If you've addressed these points, you're in good shape and can skim the rest of this chapter. If not, read on and create a high-priority plan for fixing anything awry.

There is plenty more information online if you need a deep-dive on these subjects. This is the most technically complex chapter, and my objectives are: (a) make sure you understand the importance of these fundamentals, and (b) give you enough information so you can manage the process, ask the right questions, and verify the quality of work done.

1. HTTPS

Hypertext Transfer Protocol Secure (HTTPS) is a combination of Hypertext Transfer Protocol (HTTP) and Secure Socket Layer (SSL)/Transport Layer Security (TLS). For all practical purposes, you can consider HTTPS an extension of HTTP: it is used to secure communication over the internet.

Why HTTPS is important

Governments around the world are putting all the big tech companies under pressure to improve internet safety for all users. HTTPS is an important part of the solution: it secures user data during transit, and users view HTTPS sites as being more trustworthy.

In 2014, Google offered a carrot to encourage HTTPS migration by announcing that sites moving to HTTPS would experience a "minor ranking boost". In 2016, the company added a subtle, yet stronger, message to their guidance notes, "HTTPS and making sure your site is secure is an imperative at this point".

Towards the end of 2017, the carrot became a stick as Google's Chrome browser (and others) started tagging HTTP pages as 'Not Secure'. Google's Transparency Report from April 2021 states, "Our goal is to achieve 100% encryption across our products and services".

In summary, Google is super-serious about wanting you to implement HTTPS. If you haven't migrated your website yet, this should be your number one technical project.

When I conducted the first Worldwide Digital Footprint survey in 2017, approximately 50% of the survey population had not migrated to HTTPS. The situation has improved with each successive survey, and the 2021 results reported that just 30% of surveyed sites had not implemented HTTPS. In geographic terms, the UK and European countries report a significantly higher percentage of HTTPS implementation compared with the USA.

Be careful when redirecting traffic

Google views HTTP and HTTPS addresses as totally different. To be clear, it sees no connection between the two URLs. For example:

Google views
http://www.exactdomain.com
As a completely different URL from
https://www.exactdomain.com

Here's how this seemingly subtle point could have a big impact. Suppose, over many years, you had built up a large volume of organic traffic on this domain: http://www.exactdomain.com

You decide it's time to implement HTTPS and crack on without further thought, creating: https://www.exactdomain.com

You're feeling pretty pleased with yourself until you look at your traffic figures and see the volume of traffic to your site has crashed. Why's that? Because Google is sending traffic to pages that no longer exist. For example, this page:

http://www.exactdomain.com/blog/interesting-post

…is now a dead-end. You created a new URL for it:

https://www.exactdomain.com/blog/interesting-post

…but you didn't tell Google.

To fix this, you want Google to permanently redirect all the traffic being sent to the original (non-secure) URLs to the new (secure) URLs. In internet jargon, you do this via a '301 permanent redirect'. (The precise implementation will vary according to your website. Just make sure your technical team has this covered.)

Another use for permanent redirects

If you decide to delete outdated pages in your process of redirecting to HTTPS, make sure you redirect the URL for any deleted pages to an existing page. For example, if you decide to withdraw Product A, there's little point in migrating any Product A pages to HTTPS. But you need to do something with these HTTP pages:

http://www.exactdomain.com/product-A-description
http://www.exactdomain.com/product-A-configuration
http://www.exactdomain.com/product-A-implementation-plan

If you don't redirect these URLs *somewhere*, anyone who uses a previously saved bookmark will be met with a dead-end (a '404 error'). This poor user experience could lead you to lose business. It would be better to implement 301 redirects for all the above pages, pointing them to an explanatory page. For example:

https://www.exactdomain.com/product-A-withdrawn

NUTSHELL NOTE #5 – HTTPS & 301 REDIRECT

Ensure all non-secure (HTTP) URLs are permanently redirected to their secure (HTTPS) equivalents. Test well to catch any dead links.

---

2. Mobile Experience

The 2020 edition of the Worldwide Digital Footprint survey reported that 24% of websites failed to offer a good mobile experience. A year later, that number had improved to 18%. However, that's still not good enough, here's why.

Mobile experience came to the fore when Google's trend data revealed a steep increase in the volume of traffic being served to mobile devices. Up to that point, Google's index had been based on the desktop version of your website. The company's 'mobile-first indexing policy' has changed that. Some important points:

There is no separate mobile index. This is an important point (and the source of some early confusion). In 2018, Google clarified that the mobile-first index was a change in indexing policy (not a separate index). The company stressed that the mobile version of websites would become the basis of their index.

Delayed rollout. Google announced the rollout at the end of 2017. By mid-2020, the company stated that although they had moved many sites to mobile indexing, there remained many on their 'to do' list. As part of the same announcement, they delayed the switch over from September 2020 to March 2021. In November 2021, Google removed its self-imposed deadline and no longer has a specific end date for the rollout.

Impact on new websites. Google enabled mobile-first indexing for all sites that went live after 01 July 2019.

Responsive versus adaptive web design

You will come across these two terms and ought to understand the difference between them.

Responsive websites: In a responsive website, the same content is sent to all devices and rearranged on the device in the most optimal manner. The device browser rearranges the content to deliver the best experience. Because the same content is sent to all devices, one content-management process can manage all the content.

Adaptive websites: In adaptive sites, potentially different content is sent to each device, depending on that device's capabilities. An adaptive approach utilizes multiple fixed layout sizes. The website detects the capability of the device and sends the most suitable layout. The different layouts may have the same or different content. This means you might end up having to manage multiple content streams for different devices.

Know that these two approaches exist, as you might end up having a conversation about them with your website team. Here are some additional considerations to help you prepare for that conversation.

With a responsive site, you only have one set of content to maintain. Having an adaptive site could cause you to have three sets of content: desktop, mobile, and tablet (for example). That's many more files to keep in step with one another. Do you really need the additional hassle?

There is one area where having an adaptive site could be worth the additional management overhead, and that's dealing with video headers.

Video and mobile websites

In my experience, website owners who love full-width video headers either work with animals (e.g. vets) or spend a lot of time on stage (e.g. speakers, musicians). They believe a full-width video of them 'at work' is a major contribution to their marketing.

I'm not so easily persuaded. Full-width video headers need careful planning. Even if your video editor prepares a super-lightweight version of the video, it still significantly increases the size of the homepage. This increases the download time—a definite negative impact on user experience. Full-width header videos can work for desktop sites with a good internet connection, but not for mobile sites. For mobile sites, I strongly caution you against having a full-width video header. I know they look nice (on a desktop), but I've not met one that fulfilled a vital business need. Overall, they are more trouble than they are worth. Here's why:

1. You need to create a special 'lightweight' edit of the video. I'd rather spend that money on content that delivers a stronger message to my visitors.

2. Overlaying your key message on the video is the only way to keep it 'above the fold'. The video playing underneath your message can play havoc with the visibility of the text and render it illegible to your visitors. Not good.

3. You need to create an adaptive configuration, restricting your video header to desktop sites, while an alternative page with a static header is sent to mobile devices. This gives you two different home pages to manage—and something else that can go wrong. Too much hassle for too little reward.

4. If you go down the route of having a full-width header video for your desktop visitors, commit yourself to providing a static alternative for mobile devices. But that raises this question: If a static header is good enough for mobile visitors, why isn't it good enough for all your visitors?

Overall, my recommendation is to keep life simple: have a static header with a strong headline that you serve to all visitors, no matter their device. Put your videos elsewhere on the site, where load time isn't so critical.

Provide the same experience across all devices

Google is keen for website owners to provide the same experience via desktop and mobile. Sites that don't do this will experience a drop in traffic. This is to discourage owners who were hoping to make life easy for themselves by building lightweight mobile sites that contain less content than their desktop equivalents. If Google is only indexing the mobile version of a site, it can only deliver traffic based on that mobile content. That renders additional content on the desktop site irrelevant.

The summary is clear: you should have all your content available to all visitors, regardless of how they access your site.

Google provides plenty of easily found information on best practices in this area[10]. You can test the mobile friendliness of your site using this free Google tool:

https://search.google.com/test/mobile-friendly

Top mistakes according to Google

Google has identified these common mistakes website owners make when servicing the needs of mobile users.

1. **Forgetting about the mobile community in its entirety**. It seems amazing that in the third decade of the 21st century, Google should identify such a basic error as being 'common'. However Google's finding agrees with our Worldwide Digital Footprint Survey. 18% of websites we looked at provided a poor mobile experience. To avoid falling into this category, insist your website is tested on both desktop and mobile devices. This will increase the testing workload and will drive up your development costs, but this is the price you pay for operating in today's world.

2. **Implementing a mobile site on a different domain**. Google recommends responsive web design for configuring your mobile site. It's technically possible to implement a 'special' mobile website via some other URL, but this creates a raft of complexities when it comes to updating content and keeping the two sites in step with one another. It's not clear to me why anyone would want to do this, however Google is highlighting it as a common mistake, so be aware that someone might suggest this. It's not a good idea, don't go along with it.

10 Here's a good place to start: https://developers.google.com/search/mobile-sites/get-started

NUTSHELL NOTE #6—MOBILE

Delivering a good mobile experience is vital (it's the only version of your website Google indexes). Deliver all your content to all your website visitors (regardless of their device).

3. Google's Core Web Vitals

Google announced Core Web Vitals (CWV) in May 2020 and began rolling it out in mid-2021. CWV introduces some new website ranking factors and has some overlap with mobile-first indexing.

Core Web Vitals comprise three metrics, all of which focus on user experience. According to Google, CWV are "real-world metrics" that help "quantify the user experience".

Prior to its announcement of Core Web Vitals, Google assessed a user's experience of your website by answering the following questions:

- Is this website page mobile-friendly?

- Does it provide a safe browsing experience?

- Is HTTPS enabled?

- Do any intrusive adverts appear during page load?

Core Web Vitals are new factors, so there may still be more changes coming as Google gets more experience. However, there are now three additional mid-ranking factors to consider: loading, interactivity, and visual stability.

Loading

The focus of this metric is load speed. Although developers have long considered load speed to be an important factor, Google is now confirming this and placing it in order with all the other ranking factors. Designers and developers now have more precise design criteria to guide them.

Google has identified a metric called the 'Largest Contentful Paint'. Simplistically, this indicates how quickly the main content of a webpage loads[11]. We all know from watching websites load, they don't just appear in a flash, but in a sequence of discrete 'loads'. Google wants the Largest Contentful Paint on the screen no more than 2.5s after the page load starts.

Interactivity

A period of time passes between you clicking on a button (or menu option) and the browser being able to act on the click. Google calls this the 'first input delay', and they want it to be less than 100ms (milliseconds).

To be clear: Google is not saying your whole website must have responded within 100ms. They want the time between a button click and the browser dealing with that click to be less than 100ms.

Visual Stability

You're watching a website downloading, and you already see the button you want to click. In anticipation, you move your mouse or finger to click that button, and you're just about to click it when another bit of the page arrives, and the button moves somewhere else on the screen. Before you know it, you've clicked on the wrong bit of the screen and have to start again. That's an example of visual instability.

---

11   More precisely, LCP is the time between a user triggering a page load and the largest image or text block rendering in the viewport.

Google calls this movement around the screen during page load the 'Cumulative Layout Shift', and they want it to be less than 0.1 compared to both its original position and the size of the screen. Google wants pages to be stable during load.

So what? Core Web Vitals seem fine for web designers, architects, engineers, and programmers—all of whom can now produce excellent websites that will please Google. But what does it mean for you, the owner of a website?

All other things being equal, a site optimized for CWV will rank better than one that isn't. But this isn't just about keeping Google happy. Users enjoy sites that load quickly and are stable. It's easy to see how this could lead to increased revenue by reducing abandoned shopping carts, for example.

While the introduction of Core Web Vitals is significant, it's important to keep it in context with Google's primary mission, which will always be to deliver the most relevant information to the user. Your website-creation efforts should focus on producing high-quality relevant content. When you have that, Google can provide you with clear guidelines on how to best deliver it.

4. Optimizing Website Meta Tags

Meta tags are found within the HTML code of your website and help search engines better understand how your website relates to other sites. There are different meta tags, and not all are visible to site visitors. However, they are all important to search engines and can improve your rankings in multiple ways. They tell search engines what each page is about, and they help visitors find specific pages easily.

This introduction will help you work with your website support team to verify that they've optimized your site's five important meta tags.

1. Title tag

The title tag specifies what the webpage is about and is an important on-page SEO signal. Title tags are visible in search returns and browser tabs. They are important to both visitors and search engines. Top tips:

- Ensure your title tags are placed in the <head> section of webpages

- Use unique title tags for each page of your website

- Although not a precise limit, consider 60 characters as maximum

- Use the target keyword within the tag and, if possible, at the start

- Describe the page content, e.g. How to…, Top tips for…, Review of…

- Use long-tail keywords (to help optimize the page), e.g. 'How to bake the perfect sourdough loaf'

- Use numbers, e.g. 'Top 3 ways to improve your cash flow'

2. Meta description

The title tag and meta description are equally important. The meta description is the small amount of text that appears in search returns, immediately under the title tag. Google states that the meta description is not a ranking factor. However, potential visitors will read your meta description, so its purpose is to trigger click-through to your webpage.

In recent years Google has experimented with allowing different lengths for meta descriptions. This has generated some confusion.

At the time of writing, Google advises the optimum length for meta descriptions to be 150–165 characters.

Take the time to create sharp, appealing copy, including your keywords (and special offers, if you have any). Remember, the meta description is all about click-through—you're sending a message directly to a potential site visitor.

3. Robots meta tag

The robots meta tag tells search engines which of your webpages they should index. Be careful not to confuse it with the 'robots.txt' file, which has a similar function. The robots.txt file is used to prevent sections of a site from being indexed. The robots meta tag is used to prevent individual pages from being indexed.

You can use this tag to control how search engine bots crawl your site and how they process pages. For example, consider a discontinued product. You might want to keep information about it online, so you can email webpage links to existing customers wanting service information, etc. However, you want to stop Google from indexing these pages, so you don't confuse potential new customers with information about a product you no longer sell.

4. Alt text tag

The alternative (alt) text tag describes an image. It has three uses: as a replacement for an image (if the image cannot be displayed), as the basis for an audio description of an image (for visually impaired users), and finally, to tell search engines what the image represents, since search engines can't read images.

Optimizing your images gives you another way of ranking in search results, so this tag is worth some attention. You should include keywords without going overboard. Think how you describe an image over the phone and in context with the conversation. For example, if the page relates to a local town, the alt tag might be, 'Banks Road looking south, showing the newsagents on the left and the supermarket on the right'. The same image might be described differently on a page related to proposed changes in parking regulations, 'Banks Road, showing cars parked on both sides, in contravention of parking regulations'. Write text that would make sense if read by screen-reading software, for a visually impaired visitor.

5. Canonical tag

This is important and relates to concerns over duplicate content. Starting with the term itself, Google's definition of a 'canonical URL' (from Search Console Help) gives some helpful background:

> *A canonical URL* is the URL of the best representative page from a group of duplicate pages.

The same entry goes on to say:

- Google can only index the canonical URL from a set of duplicate pages.

- A duplicate can be in a different domain than its canonical.

Say you have a great blogpost that's getting a lot of attention and you decide to 'socialize' it some more by copying it to your Medium account. This action creates a duplicate-content problem for the search engines. Sure, more people see your post, so human visitors are happy, but the search engines are confused. They see two sets of content getting a lot of attention: who do they credit as the authoritative source?

Left unresolved, the rankings of both pieces of content will suffer—the very opposite of what you intended. The canonical tag fixes this problem by telling the search engines which (of the maybe several copies) is the authoritative source. Your wider human audience can access whichever copy they like, and the search engines know how to credit the authoritative source: both audiences—humans and Google—are satisfied.

6. Keywords meta tag

Google retired this tag many years ago and you no longer need to give it any attention, but it's worth mentioning here in case you come across it.

It's easy to get lost in endless techy tweaking just for the sake of it. Focus on getting these basics boxed off and you'll have a solid foundation for any future enhancements Google and gang bring your way.

NUTSHELL NOTE #7

Build your website on solid foundations by making sure these four areas are well configured:

- HTTPS (website security)
- Mobile experience
- Google Core Web Vitals
- Optimized Metadata

6.

Finding Out More About Your Site Visitors

You can skip this chapter if you can say—with hand on heart— that you know (a) the terms *website traffic* and *visitor journeys*, (b) understand the differences between them, and (c) actively track both. If *visitor journey* is a new concept, this chapter will be worth your time. Having read it, you might even decide to introduce a new management and reporting regime.

You can perform an in-depth analysis of your website traffic using Google Analytics (my colleagues are doing it for a client as I write). It's detailed work, requiring specialist knowledge, as Analytics is such a powerful and complex product. For getting insight into many high-level marketing issues, Analytics is a sledgehammer to crack a nut, and its complexity overwhelms many website owners. While it's great to know you can call on this level of analysis capability, Google Analytics provides way more than the average business owner needs. Expect your SEO specialist to use Google Analytics and Google Search Console, but you probably don't need to spend so much time with it. My objective is to help you use specialists to meet the needs of your business, not to convert you into expert users of traffic analysis tools.

Google Analytics reports two headline metrics that are useful and easy to access: *pageviews* and *visitor sessions*:

Pageviews counts the number of times a page has been seen— including repeat views by the same visitor.

Visitor session measures the time a visitor is on your site. Sessions can include several pageviews.

You might also come across **unique pageviews**, which accounts for repeated pageviews by the same user during the same session.

For example, if a user views the same page eight times in the same session, this will generate eight pageviews. However, the same user has only generated one unique pageview, because they loaded the same page multiple times during one session. For this reason, the total pageview count will always be greater than the total number of unique pageviews (over the same time period).

Useful Google Analytics Geek-Speak

Google Analytics is so popular, you are bound to come across it, even if only in conversation. As such, it's worth mentioning a few more points, so if your technical team does a deep dive into geek-speak, you can remain engaged and ensure the conversation meets your business needs.

Bounce rate

Google has used this metric for many years to measure the percentage of visitors who leave a website after viewing only one page (the one on which they landed). This needs a lot of interpretation to be useful. For example, a visitor could spend ages reading one fascinating blogpost, which means, although very engaged, their session would still count as a bounce. Google realizes this and intends to retire bounce rate in July 2023, replacing it with a new metric called *engagement rate*.

The new engagement rate metric will be much more useful, as it will measure sessions that:

- last 10 seconds or longer

- have at least one *conversion event* (see below)

- have a minimum of two pageviews

Conversion events

Google gives you control over how you define conversion events for your website. Typically, you'll want to pick an action that is valuable to your business. Clearly, product purchase via your online store would be valuable and would certainly be a good conversion event. But so would other marketing initiatives that might not directly have a monetary value. This could include a visitor signing up for a lead magnet, watching a video, or reading product descriptions or reviews.

In summary, from mid-2023 bounce rate will be replaced by a metric that's far more useful for tracking marketing activities. To take advantage of it, document the events your website visitors experience on their journey from being a first-time, unknown visitor through to being a loyal client. Your technical team can configure Google Analytics to track these events. This will give you valuable insight into how visitors use your website.

Google Analytics 4 upgrade

Your Google Analytics account tracks your website traffic by receiving data from code that you (or your tech team) place on your website. Google has updated the code over the years. In October 2020, Google launched Analytics 4 (GA4) as a replacement for all previous versions (referred to as Universal Analytics).

Google will stop processing all data from Universal Analytics on 01 July 2023. In other words, they are forcing everyone to move to GA4. This is one of those tasks that needs to be done, so ask your tech team to handle this for you. (Google has created a GA4 Setup Assistant[12] to help site owners with the migration.)

12 https://support.google.com/analytics/answer/9744165

Where to get help with Google Analytics

I'm not suggesting you convert yourself into an Analytics specialist. You have a business to run, and life is too short. You need to know enough to get the help you need (and know if you're being sold a line).

There is a lot of help available online. If I've piqued your interest and you want to know more, a good place to start is the Google Analytics Academy:

Google Analytics for Beginners

https://analytics.google.com/analytics/academy/course/6

This course only addresses Universal Analytics, so it will be out of date by mid-2023.

Google Analytics 4

https://skillshop.exceedlms.com/student/catalog/list?category_ids=6431-google-analytics-4

Google created Skillshop as a one-stop-shop for all Google tools, products, etc. The site has a good search facility and contains excellent material. The link above will take you to GA4 materials.

Tracking Visitor Journeys and Behaviour

The concept of visitor journeys (and our ability to track them) is newer than our ability to track pageviews and sessions. Once business owners understand visitor journeys, they're quick to see the business value.

Imagine you have connected a tool like Google Analytics to a piano keyboard (stick with me, this exercise will make sense). The tool could tell you many intricate details. For example, when the pianist strikes a key, the tool could tell you whether the note was in tune, the pressure exerted on the keys, the duration each key was depressed, the pedal positions associated with each key depression, and much more. In other words, it would provide lots of highly detailed information that would be useful to piano makers who want to build a better piano or piano tuners who want to tune the piano for a special rendition.

But what if you don't make musical instruments and don't need all this detail? What if you simply want to know who's playing the piano and what tune they are playing? This is similar to the visitor-journey concept. Who approached the piano? Did they just look at it, or did they sit down and play? How long did they play? How many tunes did they play, and what were they? Did they play really well, or fluff up a few notes here and there?

The difference? The first set of data is about the physics and mechanics of the piano. The second set is about who is playing the piano and how they play it. You need tools that can provide you with both sets of data.

Let's get back to your website. There are five key questions you ought to have in mind when discussing traffic and content:

- Are my visitors seeing the important content?

- Are they clicking where I want them to?

- To what degree are they distracted?

- Is any non-clickable content causing confusion?

- Are they getting an equally enjoyable experience across all devices?

The first four questions are concerned with the behaviour of visitors during their journeys through your website. (You can answer the last question using the information from the previous chapter.)

Figure 6-1 illustrates a typical user journey, to help you visualize how journeys and behaviours differ from pageviews and sessions.

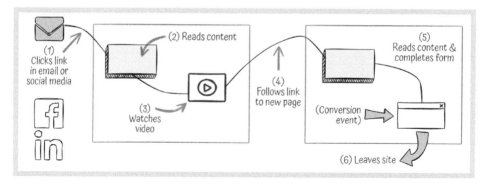

Figure 6-1: Visitor journeys and behaviour analysis focus on how visitors move through and interact with a website.

1. The user clicks a link in an email, for example, or a social media post.

2. The link directs them to a website page (triggering a pageview count and starting the session timer).

3. The visitor watches a video that's part of the content they are consuming.

4. Sufficiently impressed, they click on another link and are taken to another page (triggering another pageview).

5. They read the information on this page and decide to complete the form (triggering a conversion event).

6. They leave the site and the session timer stops.

Behaviour-analysis and visitor-tracking tools

All the tools introduced in this next section were announced between 2014 and 2018—more than a decade after Google's initial release of Analytics in 2005. Visitor journey and behaviour analysis is a rapidly developing market, so I'm going to focus on approaches and outcomes, skipping transient technical details. All three tools introduced below offer something slightly different. Used together with Google's tools they will give you a comprehensive view of your website visitors.

Funnelytics

Canadian entrepreneur and marketeer Mikael Dia launched Funnelytics in 2018, partly from his own frustration with deriving valuable marketing material from existing tools, such as Google Analytics.

In a brief space of time, the Funnelytics team has developed a remarkable tool that adopts an intuitive and novel two-step approach.

The first step taps into how much easier it is for us to understand websites if we can see a flowchart or diagram—a bit like Figure 6-1 you've just viewed. You can use Funnelytics to create this sort of diagram. Used in this mode, Funnelytics performs as a specialized drawing package, akin to a mashup between Miro, PowerPoint, and AutoCAD, for example.

The second step reveals the tool's superpower. With just a few keystrokes, you're able to make the drawing of your website 'live' by connecting it to the internet and watching how traffic moves through all the pages of your site.

Funnelytics is a beautiful tool for showing business owners how visitors interact with their website. It's easy to see how visitors arrive, the popular pages they visit, where they go next, and finally, where they exit the site.

In summary, Funnelytics allows you to:

- Sketch a website layout, showing all the pages and connections between them.

- Connect real page URLs for existing sites to the layout and see how traffic flows through the site.

- Calculate advanced measurements, such as scroll depth and button clicks on individual pages.

I'm happy to declare an interest and say that I was one of the early investors in Funnelytics. We use the tool at Active Presence to underpin our Website Value Scan (WVS) consulting service.

https://funnelytics.io
https://chrisdavidson.co.uk/wvs

Hotjar

Hotjar's aim is to help you keep people on your website for as long as possible. For example, it can detect parts of your site that aren't attracting attention so you can redesign or remove them.

Hotjar's heatmaps locate the most activity on each webpage. You can quickly discover the parts of your site visitors find interesting and the areas they skip over. For example, suppose your website lists services by 'category'. If the categories tab is getting lots of attention, you can reasonably presume visitors want to view your content according to your predefined categories. Another example could be scroll depth. If you combine percentage scroll depth with time spent on a page, you can estimate how engaged visitors are with your content.

You can access other Hotjar heatmaps, in addition to the scroll-heatmap, which gives you a percentage of the page scrolled. The click-heatmap illustrates where visitors click (and their click frequency), and the move-heatmap shows you where visitors are hovering their mouse.

https://hotjar.com

Microsoft Clarity

Microsoft announced Clarity in 2018, with full public access from the end of October 2020. Hotjar launched in 2014, making Microsoft the new kid on the block. Microsoft's approach to pricing Clarity makes it worthy of mention, as it looks as if the firm wants to shake up the market in the same way Google did with Analytics.

Clarity is probably causing consternation at Hotjar headquarters. Although (at time of writing) Hotjar offers a free restricted-function licence, the tool's full capabilities are only accessible via a monthly subscription. In stark contrast, Microsoft announced Clarity as 'free forever'.

Clarity offers heatmaps, session recordings, and connection with Google Analytics. Some Hotjar supporters claim that Clarity isn't as comprehensive, but Clarity is the newer tool. If you have little experience with heatmaps and tracking user interaction, dipping your toe into the water with a free tool first makes a lot of sense.

Some other tools similar to Clarity and Hotjar: Crazy Egg, MouseFlow, Inspectlet, HeatMap, and Smartlook.

https://clarity.microsoft.com

The focus of Tier 1 of the Website Effectiveness Framework is helping you create a technically cogent website. Going back to our small island community from Chapter 3, this is the equivalent to the shipwrights creating seaworthy craft. Now that you have a seaworthy website, it's time to get some passengers aboard and put out to sea.

Part D will help you engage your website visitors and start building a professional relationship with them.

NUTSHELL NOTE #8

Google Analytics is a great tool and has been around for years. Newer tools focus on the 'visitor journey' and are more useful to marketing-oriented people, including business owners.

Systems & Community Engagement (WEF Tiers 2 & 3)

7.

Why The Information Age is Yesterday's News

A precept of the Information Age is that finding information is easy. Your value comes from helping clients make use of information to solve their pressing needs. Attention spans are shortening, and niches are narrowing—gaining attention is harder than it used to be. You need to focus your marketing efforts on clients who are the best fit for what you do—while making 'what you do' explicit.

While it's true that finding information is easy, I believe there's much about the Information Age that no longer holds true. Although I know next to nothing about farming, I like to broaden my knowledge and enjoy listening to the early-morning radio show *Farming Today*. A recent episode included a piece on the use of drones within farming—something I'd never considered. The guest farmer explained how he used a drone equipped with ground-piercing radar to optimize the application of nutrients to his crops. Overflying a field, the drone's radar identified individual plants and calculated dosage requirements based on the radar image of the plant's root structure. It transmitted this data to a robot plant sprayer, which moved across the field, identifying and dosing the individual plants according to data supplied by the drone.

What a fascinating niche application of technology and, on the face of it, an example of the modern Information Age we come across in the general press, on TV, etc.

This installment of *Farming Today* makes a great jumping-off point for further study. Let's explore the niche market of using drones within agriculture. Here's the search term I entered into Google's UK search engine:

Renting drones for commercial agricultural use

You might expect a modest number of search returns for a search as precise as this within a niche market. Not so; in under a second Google.co.uk delivered 11,600,000 search results[13]. Of course, that's far from neatly organized information. It's a vast smorgasbord of data points that somehow fit my supposedly precise search of 'renting drones for commercial agricultural use'.

There were five adverts on the first page of search returns, all relating to the specific use of drones in UK agriculture. Appearing under the adverts were these top organic search returns:

Drone Hire For Farmers
Farming & Agriculture Drones
Crop Spraying & Surveying
Drones For Agriculture 2021: The Ultimate Buyer's Guide

Imagine being a farmer faced with all these search returns. You'd have to wade your way through them and invent some process that would help you make a decision that could cost you many thousands of pounds.

---

13 From google.co.uk in October 2021 (as are the subsequent search-return examples)

With that much interest and competition in such a niche market, the first job of any company is to rise above the noise and get their message heard. It's too easy for the farmer to be distracted by another potential supplier's website, email, online brochure, video meeting, etc.

The first job is to grab the farmer's attention, draw them in and engage them in a meaningful dialogue that helps the farmer solve their problem, while demonstrating the supplier's credentials, as part of a trust-building exercise.

Based on this, we're not in the Information Age at all—that's been and gone. Your business now operates in the 'Engage Age'. This is especially true if you sell services—anything that's not a commodity. This story illustrates how competitive even niche markets can become. You can't assume that your potential client will find you and spend their valuable time working out whether you have what they want.

Time for more questions:

1. What does your website do to grab the attention of your most valuable prospects?

2. When those valuable prospects visit your website, how do you go about encouraging them to engage with your content?

3. Aside from your website, how well known are you to your target market and how easy are you to find online?

What's coming up will help you answer these questions.

NUTSHELL NOTE #9

Digital noise is drowning out your marketing messages. Focus on attracting the attention of high value prospects. Start by being clear on who your prospects are, what you can do for them, and where you can find them (online and offline).

8.

Gaining Trust and Showing Expertise and Authority

If your WEF tier 1 is in good shape, then you have a seaworthy vessel and can leave harbour with confidence. But where are you going? To whom will you speak? And about what? How will you demonstrate your expertise and gain the trust of people you meet? Answers to these questions underpin the next two tiers of the framework, so it's worth laying them out in a chapter of their own.

Reflecting on the farmer and drone story, I'm sure drone operators in the agriculture market will have asked themselves these questions. Certainly, the author of the following content wanted to gain market trust as an objective expert:

Drones For Agriculture 2021: The Ultimate Buyer's Guide

Gaining trust online, demonstrating your expertise and verifying your authority are critical steps in turning website visitors into viable leads. Luckily, this is also Google's view. To help you achieve these objectives, Google introduced the E-A-T (expertise, authority, and trustworthiness) concept in the 2014 edition of its Search Quality Guidelines and has continued to give it increasing prominence[14].

---

14 The 2021 edition of Google's Search Quality Guidelines refers to E-A-T 137 times (in fewer than 200 pages).

E-A-T is very important to Google—and hence, to you—even though it's not directly a ranking factor. Google has approximately 10,000 Search Quality Raters worldwide. Their job is to manually review the quality of webpages. Their results are used to improve the search algorithms. The reviewers use the E-A-T guidelines to study:

- The content of the webpage under review

- The website to which the page belongs

- The creator of the content

Important as E-A-T is, it's vital to keep some perspective. It's too easy to come across misleading or incorrect information online. Some people want you to believe that E-A-T is some newfangled way of ranking search results. It isn't. To ensure you're forewarned, here are some common misunderstandings. There is no such thing as an 'E-A-T score' and E-A-T itself is not an algorithm. You cannot use E-A-T to fix technical weaknesses. E-A-T operates side-by-side with other optimization techniques; it doesn't render any of them obsolete.

There are two further points to cover: the effort you should give E-A-T and what you can expect in return.

How Much Effort Should You Give E-A-T?

Google does not treat all websites the same but categorizes them according to an additional concept: 'Your Money or Your Life' (YMYL). Webpages aren't awarded a numeric YMYL score, but a low-to-high rating. E-A-T and YMYL go hand in hand and understanding where your business sits within the YMYL framework will help you decide how much effort you give E-A-T.

Content with high YMYL has the potential to affect a person's health, finances, happiness, or safety. Google's quality raters will hold such pages to a much higher E-A-T standard.

Some example content categories and likely YMYL ratings:

- Pencil sketching for beginners
  No YMYL rating

- Celebrity gossip, entertainment news, sports
  Low YMYL rating

- Information about voting, social services, child custody, etc.
  High YMYL rating

- Pet health
  High YMYL rating

- Health and safety, medical issues, drugs, hospitals, etc.
  Max YMYL rating

All ecommerce pages are high YMYL. So, if the owner of the first example, 'pencil sketching for beginners', decides to sell courses online, their ecommerce pages will automatically have a high YMYL rating, even though the main pages might not. This is a good example of where Google's quality raters have to use their judgement.

The higher you think your YMYL rating will be, the more E-A-T effort you should put into your content.

What Can You Expect in Return?

As E-A-T is not a direct ranking factor, its influence is more gradual. Building trust with users takes time, and it takes additional time for them to reflect that trust into your website—and then yet more time for it to be picked up and acted on by search engines.

Take 'pencil sketching for beginners' and assume the site has no ecommerce capabilities—it's a 'hints-and-tips' site run by an enthusiast. The owner can share their expertise without being held to account by Google's quality raters and E-A-T.

Now suppose the owner upgrades the site and offers for sale: an online group course, weekend painting retreats, and a new 1-on-1 program, 'Sketching for Advanced Artists'. The significant ecommerce content falls under YMYL and Google will hold the content to a higher E-A-T standard. For example, the quality raters might want to see clear evidence of delighted customers. They might also look more closely at the artist's biography: has the artist mentioned their Royal Academy membership or schooling at the world-renowned Glasgow School of Art? And how about the residency at the Massachusetts Institute of Technology? Is there content or backlinks verifying these claims?

Clearly, upgrading such a site from a simple hints-and-tips site will take time. And it will then take more time for the search engines to index the new content, and for it to be verified.

If Google holds your content to a high E-A-T standard, then patience is the name of the game. Focus on the high quality that your clients would expect of you, and you'll also satisfy Google and improve your search results.

NUTSHELL NOTE #10

Expertise, authority, and trustworthiness (E-A-T) are important signals for Google when assessing the quality of your website—particularly so for sites dealing with services. Your money, your life (YMYL) is an additional factor that determines the standard to which Google holds your content.

9.

Your Lead Magnets: WTF?

Weak target focus (WTF) is the most common reason for lead magnets to perform poorly. Before diving into the details of website-driven lead generation, let me set the scene with an introduction to lead magnets and sign-up forms.

The Problem Lead Magnets Solve

Most of your website visitors are not ready to buy. (There are a few exceptions, and I address them shortly.) Think back to the farmer from the previous chapter. The farmer started with some online research about drones, prior to investing many thousands of pounds into equipment or services.

Lead magnets help plug the gap between the visitor who isn't ready to commit and the one who is.

What is a lead magnet?

In short, it's some form of gated content. Typically this is material that visitors access in exchange for providing their contact details (normally name and email address) via a sign-up form.

A good lead magnet can be the start of a fruitful client/supplier relationship. A good lead magnet serves two commanders equally: the website visitor and the website owner.

For the visitor, a lead magnet should help them solve an important (or urgent) need. The more personalized the help is to their circumstances, the more value they attribute to it and the greater the trust they will place in the website owner. Signing up for a lead magnet provides a low-risk avenue for a visitor to assess a potential supplier's capabilities. A good magnet should help answer the questions, "Do I like the cut of this person's jib? Can I trust them?"

For the website owner, their lead magnet is a chance to showcase their skill and help differentiate themselves from their competitors. It's an opportunity to provide honest advice, with the genuine intent of helping the visitor solve their immediate problem. This helps position visitors who might purchase at some future point. Website visitors understand that signing up for a lead magnet will not keep the website owner fed and watered; they're not expecting the entire answer for free.

Do all businesses need lead magnets?

The vast majority, yes. The small number of businesses that can manage without include those:

- that sell directly to consumers (B2C[15]) and…

- whom clients approach when their issue reaches some critical threshold

For example, my company manages the website of a clinical psychologist who fulfils these criteria and runs a successful practice without having a lead magnet. Clients find her website either via an internet search or by clicking a link on a referring website (such as the British Psychological Society). Some clients arrive via a recommendation from a friend or family member.

Regardless of how clients come to contact the psychologist, they do so because they've reached a point where they recognize they

15 B2C: Business to consumer

need help. People in this position don't need a lead magnet. Once they find a supplier they can trust, they quickly take action.

To illustrate how circumstances could change, let's suppose the psychologist expanded her offerings and started selling to businesses (B2B[16])—a workshop on mental health, for example. The purchasing decision is now very different: the workshop participants (who receive the benefit) are a different person from the one paying. It's highly likely that the purchasing decision would involve several people, for example, procurement, HR, training, and various other heads of department. With this level of complexity, the psychologist could increase her chances of closing the sale by having supporting material available to her corporate clients when she isn't. A lead magnet would be an important part of that supporting library.

In summary, lead magnets will be useful to all businesses operating in a B2B market and most businesses operating in a B2C environment.

Essential Ingredients of a Good Lead Magnet

Weak target focus is the scourge of lead magnets, and its root lies in the false belief that more is better. The argument can be summarized as, 'The more people sign-up for my lead magnet, the bigger my email list, the greater my sales numbers'. This is faulty logic. You achieve better results if you focus on quality over quantity.

A good lead magnet encourages the right people to sign-up, while signaling that those outside your niche shouldn't bother. Achieve this by following the guidance in the next six subsections.

Clarify your target

Be brave, be precise. Don't worry about excluding people. Reducing the size of the pond you're fishing in will feel counterintuitive at first but will yield results in the long run.

16 B2B: Business to business

For example, legal and medical secretaries both have specialized skills that separate them from other secretarial or general administrative positions. If you focus on training legal and medical secretaries, your lead magnet should be useful to these specific groups, and by omission exclude people with more general secretarial skills. For example:

- *Take our test and discover whether you could handle the stress of being a medical secretary.* Good

- *Crush your next interview with our sample legal secretary interview questions.* Good

- *Improve your secretarial skills with our 10 point checklist.* WTF

The first two titles also tell your visitor that you know your onions. To create a good lead magnet that satisfies the first two titles, you must have done your research and know your market. By contrast, you could subcontract the third title to a general copywriter. While there's nothing inherently wrong with that, it's not going to attract your target market. What it will do is fill your email list with inferior-quality leads (more on that later).

Be of service first

This is a subtle, but important, point—and one that's not been exploited by many site owners. If you're an early reader, you're in the vanguard, so the quicker you act, the better.

There are two related benefits; one helps you build trust with your site visitor, the other improves your content from an E-A-T perspective.

Here's an overview of the process underpinning a traditional lead magnet:

- The visitor arrives on a page advertising the lead magnet

- The page contains content that persuades the visitor to complete the form

- The visitor enters their contact details (typically name and email address) and clicks the 'complete' button

- The visitor is redirected to what's called the 'thank you' page. This contains information about how they can get their lead magnet. It might be a download directly from the thank you page, or it might be emailed to the address the visitor entered.

For completeness, it's worth noting two extras. Many countries now have legislation in place governing the collection of visitor details, and you ought to comply with them. A common European standard is GDPR[17]. Some website owners use a two-step sign-up process. The first step is the website form. Completing this form triggers an email to the new registrant's email address. To complete their registration, the new registrant must click a link in this email. This two-step process ensures visitors use a genuine email address when signing up.

I don't want GDPR or the precise sign-up mechanism to cloud the main point, which is: Google cannot read all the great content in your lead magnet. In this example, your entire lead magnet is behind a sign-up form. Google's indexing bots will stop at the sign-up form, as will their human counterparts, the quality raters. If you have great E-A-T content in your lead magnet, it will only be available to visitors who sign-up.

Second point; you're asking people to take you on trust. In recent years, there has been an explosion of lead magnets of variable

17   General Data Protection Regulation, https://gdpr.eu/

quality. Many website visitors now shy away from sharing their contact details.

You can build trust by delivering value without requiring visitors to sign-up. The Website Effectiveness Assessment is an example. You may recall how you were able to complete the assessment—and get your overall website effectiveness score—without handing over any contact details. If, at that stage, you didn't feel the assessment was providing the value you were looking for, you could leave, free of any concern that I'd put your details onto an email list.

Having completed the assessment and got your overall score, I asked you if you'd like to exchange your contact details for a detailed report, giving scores for each tier of the framework.

From my perspective, this gives me the opportunity to show my expertise and add real value to a visitor's business early in a potential relationship. If the visitor doesn't want to take it any further, that's fine: I've saved the cost of storing contact details of someone who would never have become a client. The visitor leaves free from potential contact they didn't want. The best outcome for both parties. Visitors that sign-up for the full report are demonstrating interest in their business and trust in me. They get a detailed report they can use as the basis for an action plan, and I'm able to contact someone who's interested in my work. An excellent result for both parties.

Personalize the promise

The Website Effectiveness Assessment also shows how personalizing your lead magnet to your visitor's circumstances is an excellent way to show more expertise and build great trust. The more personal you make the experience, the more you'll be helping your visitor and the easier you're making it for them to trust you.

For example, 'Take our test and discover whether you could handle the stress of being a medical secretary' suggests the user will get a personalized result, giving them insights on how they might respond to the role. You can imagine this being valuable to someone considering this career path. Providing a personal score makes this lead magnet more valuable than the one that offered the same sample interview questions to all users.

Demonstrate your respect for the value inherent in your visitor's email address by offering something very specific in exchange.

Be clear about the key benefits

Be crystal clear about what's delivered and the benefits the user will get from your lead magnet. In the example of the 'medical secretary stress test', is the user getting an on-screen score, an emailed report, or both? If a report, how many pages? How was the test developed? How accurate and reliable are the results? Is the test recognized by any professional bodies? You get the picture.

Call-to-action button text

Button text is important. Joanna Wiebe, founder of Copyhackers, recommends: Have the headline (of the section where you start selling your call-to-action) and button (that people click to complete the call-to-action) in reasonable proximity to one another. Have the button text complement the headline text. Compose the button text so it completes either of the following sentences:

- *I want to…*
- *I want you to…*

Applying this to the example of the sample interviews for the legal secretary, button texts could be:

- *I want to…* Crush My Next Interview
- *I want you to…* Show Me My Sample Questions

Demonstrate your credentials and position for purchase

Your lead magnet is the first substantial content you deliver to your visitor. It changes your visitor into a lead. That's all. It doesn't change them into a raving fan or someone who's going to hit your ecommerce system with their credit card until it melts.

Many businesses mess up here. Your new lead will certainly not share the enthusiasm you have for your topic. You're one of many plates they are trying to keep spinning. They need your help, and your lead magnet must deliver it.

It's perfectly reasonable to show examples of how you've helped clients in similar circumstances (this further builds trust and demonstrates your expertise). It's reasonable to tell them more about you and the background to your work and approach (thus communicating authority).

Save the sales pitch for when you've qualified your new lead and have something specific to offer.

Where to Start

By now you'll realize I'm in favour of assessment-based lead magnets. They do an excellent job of qualifying website visitors. People willing to invest their time in completing an assessment are more likely to be interested in your services. You have two challenges, the first of which is to create an assessment that would help your perfect client solve a pressing issue.

The second challenge is to put your new assessment online, following the earlier model. First, a free personalized response (offered without any need to sign-up). Then an optional detailed report for visitors who want more help. Those who sign-up for the report are viable leads, worthy of further contact.

A significant part of the challenge is choosing what software to use from the vast range available. There aren't many software services that combine good online assessment capability with the production of PDF reports. We were so impressed by Pointerpro that we use it at Active Presence to underpin our Website Content Engager service[18].

Ditch the Dead Wood

Lead magnets based on questionnaires collect valuable information about the lead. Expect fewer leads of higher quality. Visitors with a low level of interest won't bother completing an assessment. Those that do have shown enough interest to qualify themselves as a viable lead. When visitors complete your questionnaire, they also give you information you can use in qualifying the opportunity they present.

We all have the continual challenge of clearing out the dead wood from our email list. That dead wood is our own fault. We've encouraged it over the years by offering generic information that visitors found useful enough to surrender an email address—even though they had no intent of ever becoming a client.

Visitors have become savvier about how website owners use their information, with many visitors providing email addresses they use only for accessing free content. There are hundreds of thousands of email lists out there stuffed to the gills with duff emails— people who are never going to give you money or recommend you strongly to their network.

The email providers count this 'subscribed but disengaged' population within your overall subscriber count and delight in hitting your credit card every month on this basis. This does more damage than just unnecessarily inflating your expenses. Members of your list who are 'subscribed and disengaged' damage your email open rates and ultimately, your domain's sender reputation. You should ditch these people.

---

18 https://pointerpro.com and https://chrisdavidson.co.uk/website-content-engager

Focus on those who are engaged (i.e. those who read your emails) and ditch the rest. And then alter your whole engagement strategy to encourage subscriptions from those who are more likely to be genuinely interested in what you offer. You're the expert in your market. You know what bugs people. You know what they're struggling with. Drive a truck full of value down that road and see who flags you down.

NUTSHELL NOTE #11

Lead magnets are important for most websites. Personalize yours to the user's individual circumstances and help them solve a pressing need. Offer some help without any requirement to sign-up.

Part E

P-CAM
User Guide
(WEF Tier 4)

10.

The Product-Client Alignment Matrix (P-CAM)

Just as Shakespeare's *Hamlet* is a play-within-a-play, this entire section is a book-within-a-book. The next three chapters are the user guide for the Product-Client Alignment Matrix (P-CAM), the software tool that comes as part of *Why Your Website Doesn't Work*. Brief answers to some common questions:

What Problem Does P-CAM Solve?

The tool helps you create product-oriented copy for websites (and elsewhere). It helps business owners who struggle to clearly state what they do and for whom. In my experience, this is most common in the services sector. It's as if business owners haven't asked themselves, "What does this do for my clients? What need does this satisfy?"

What is P-CAM?

P-CAM is a spreadsheet-based text-processing tool. Owners of *Why Your Website Doesn't Work* can download a fully functioning copy for free. You're reading the user guide right now.

What Does P-CAM Do?

P-CAM helps you more closely align your product descriptions to your clients' most pressing needs. It's designed to help you and guide you. It's not a magic wand; you need to do the work. In summary, P-CAM helps in the following four areas:

Perfect client: P-CAM helps you define your perfect client more precisely, particularly with regards to their pressing needs and what might be holding them back.

Product descriptions: Starting from an outline, P-CAM helps you create more engaging and helpful descriptions for your products (e.g. workshops, online courses, one-to-one coaching, etc.).

Message optimization: Clients don't just decide to buy your stuff: they go on a journey of several waypoints. When they decide to fix a problem, they most likely don't know who you are or how you could help them. They research the market, discover you, learn more about what you do, etc. P-CAM helps you deliver a message optimized to each waypoint of your client's journey.

E-A-T: The tool acts as a prompt for satisfying Google's E-A-T requirements.

Is P-CAM Part of WEF?

P-CAM is a tool that sits alongside the Website Effectiveness Framework. Its purpose is to help the many business owners who get stuck at the framework's fourth tier, Market Alignment.

This part of the book has a distinct style from the rest. It's a software user guide and I recommend you have P-CAM open as you study these chapters.

If you haven't already done so, download your copy of P-CAM from:

https://chrisdavidson.co.uk/get-p-cam

To use P-CAM effectively, you need to both understand how the tool works and think very deeply about your business and clients.

Previous users of P-CAM have found this useful and rewarding, as well as involved and challenging. P-CAM access is reserved to those who have the user guide (this book). To access P-CAM, you will need to prove that you've purchased the book. P-CAM is a software tool and software never sits still, so we need to be able to contact you about future P-CAM updates if needed.

Software and Skill Prerequisites

To get the best experience run P-CAM on a desktop computer with a reasonable screen size. You will need a machine running Microsoft Excel 2010 or later.

You will need basic Excel editing skills, for example, selecting a cell, entering text, changing the height of a row. (You do not need to know advanced Excel functions or how to use formulae.)

P-CAM Workflow

Ever stepped on a stray piece of LEGO barefooted? P-CAM helps you organize your building blocks a whole pile better.

Although P-CAM is one tool, you use different parts of it in a natural sequence to achieve different objectives.

Step 1: You record details of your *niche market* and the *perfect client* for that niche. Chapter 11 (next) gives you step-by-step instructions. Clients frequently tell me that going through the disciplined process of putting all this information in one place is itself hugely beneficial, clarifying, and energizing.

Step 2: In this output step, P-CAM presents you with *transformation statements* based on Step 1. These should set your synapses firing with new ideas about how you could help your perfect clients. More on transformation statements in the next chapter.

Step3: You now have a clear definition of your perfect client and some ideas on how you can help them. Chapter 12 tells you how you can use this insight with guidance from P-CAM to create *offers* and *products* that address your perfect clients' pressing needs.

P-CAM Layout

P-CAM is an Excel spreadsheet workbook with seven tabs, five of which need your input. The tabs are both numbered and named. You should complete them in sequence, from left to right, as entries in earlier tabs are used in later tabs.

Each tab contains differing numbers of tables, and each table has a unique alphanumeric name. For example, Table 3a is the first table on the third tab, while Table 4c is the third table on the fourth tab.

Here are the names of the tabs and a summary for each, as laid out from left to right in the workbook.

Cover

This is the title page. It contains version-level information and product notes.

1-Niche

This is an input tab containing one table. Its purpose is to clarify the niche you're serving. (See Chapter 11 for details.)

2-Client

This is also an input tab. Its two tables are used to define your perfect client. (See Chapter 11 for details.)

3-Transformation

This is an output tab. There is one table, its content automatically generated by P-CAM. You use this output as a reference when defining your products.

4-O&P-Primary

O&P stands for 'Offers & Products'. There are three O&P tabs, all with similar layouts. They are all product-definition templates.

Your 'primary' product is one you want to sell the most. Normally, it's your biggest revenue generator or most profitable product. (See Chapter 12 for details.)

5-O&P-Secondary

In summary, your secondary product is what you sell when your client can't afford your primary product.

6-O&P-Tertiary

Your tertiary product is typically a trial product—a low cost, entry product a client could purchase as a way to test you out.

P-CAM Data Input and Colour Coding

The input and output cells have colour-coded backgrounds:

- **Light Grey**
  Treat these cells as a notepad. Content you enter here is not used elsewhere

- **Light Blue**
  Input cells—all content you enter in these cells is used elsewhere

- **Pale Green**
  Select a response from the cell's drop-down menu

- **Pale Yellow**
  You cannot edit the content of these cells (it's been generated by P-CAM)

In summary, you need to complete the blue cells and select a response from the green ones.

The next chapter contains detailed instructions on using P-CAM to define your perfect client.

NUTSHELL NOTE #12

The Product-Client Alignment Matrix (P-CAM) helps you create better product-oriented copy for your website. It's a tool that acts as a repository and method of organization for your thoughts. It saves you time and improves the quality of your website.

11.

Using P-CAM to Define Your Perfect Client

This chapter addresses Tabs 1 to 3 of P-CAM.

Tabs 4 to 6 are covered in Chapter 12.

At some point in our lives, I'm sure we've all struggled to find the right words. Possibly romantically, perhaps in sympathy, or maybe more mundanely, failing to deliver a clear set of directions to someone trying to find their way to the local pub. Words matter. Why should it be any different with websites?

Maybe you've been lulled into believing words matter less than gorgeous graphics, cool animated slider-thingies, and intricate conversations about the delicacy of this font versus that one. Forget all this for the moment. I'm not saying this stuff isn't valuable, but I see too many people giving it too much focus at the wrong time.

First, get your message right. Then let that feed the visual aspects of the design process. Fonts and graphics don't lead your client's decision process. Clients decide whether they want to work with you based on the promise you make them. That promise needs to be written in words your client can read, understand, and interpret for their situation.

This is true even for heavily visual service sectors (like graphic design or photography). Sure, an arresting graphic design can draw someone in. But reading about how the designer works, what their discovery process is, how they communicate with their clients, what their creative milestones are—it's all this that helps the client decide whether the designer makes it onto the shortlist.

Many business owners get stuck at this point. Their sites lack enough content of sufficient depth and quality to engage visitors and lead them to wanting more. There are two main reasons for this failing: business owners not understanding in sufficient detail *who* their perfect client is and what their *needs* are.

This chapter is about the first point: defining your perfect client. Some business owners use the term dream client, but I don't find that helpful. Dreams aren't real; they're a figment of your unconscious imagination: not a good basis for any business, in my view.

I want to keep the issue grounded in reality, so I prefer the term *perfect* client. The client who is such a great fit for what you do (and the way you do it) that you'd be happy to clone them and serve only them until your days are done.

You have options as to how you use your P-CAM output. Some of our clients use it to write tighter and deeper copy for their websites, while others use it to brief a copywriter to do the job for them.

There is one other important reason for investing time and effort in defining your perfect client. The target market defined by your perfect client should get the lion's share of your marketing budget. Prospects who aren't 'perfect' will appear from time-to-time, caught in the wake of your marketing campaigns. You can decide whether (and how) to service these less-than-perfect 'drag-along' opportunities as and when they appear. The point is: you shouldn't knowingly spend time or money on attracting less-than-perfect potential clients.

P-CAM Exemplar

Your P-CAM workbook comes complete with a worked example referenced throughout this guide. Here are some important points about the exemplar case study and pre-loaded content.

The exemplar is a work of fiction whose sole purpose is to illustrate how P-CAM works. It's not based on a fully thought-through business case, so please don't respond to it as if it were. Specifically, don't base any decisions for your business on the pre-loaded content. Use the exemplar to learn how the tool works, and then enter data relevant to your own business and circumstances.

Characters

Alison Tan	– Business owner and P-CAM user
Yusuf Aydin	– Alison's perfect client
Jim Medlock,	
Pauline Morris,	
Sheri Cheesman	– Some of Alison's other clients

Background

Alison Tan has worked in the human resources arena for 35 years, running her own company for the past 14 years. She started her career in HR operations and then moved into recruitment. Alison enjoyed a lot of success as a headhunter, placing people into well-paid, corporate jobs. She took this forward into her own business and added a formal coaching qualification to upgrade the service she delivered to individual and corporate clients. Alison tracks the careers of the people she has placed and stays close to the most successful. They frequently use Alison when recruiting team members, as their own careers progress. This expands Alison's network and gives her a fresh supply of new clients.

The COVID-19 pandemic took its toll on many companies. Enforced temporary measures became the new normal, and many furloughed employees found their positions declared redundant. Large-scale reorganizations left many executive managers feeling exposed as companies downsized and redeployed their remaining workforce.

Those that sensed the change in the wind started considering alternative streams of income. Some thought about establishing a small portfolio of non-executive directorships (NED). This would give them exposure to other companies, build their c.v., broaden their experience, and provide a financial cushion should their main employment fail. Working against them is their relative youth and inexperience when compared with the view many people have of the typical non-exec: someone around retirement age, with lots of experience built up in different companies over a long, successful career.

Many company boards recognize times have changed and technology has a permanent and much greater role to play in how they deliver value to their clients. Executive managers are asking their boards for more support in this area, and many boards feel unable to respond confidently and competently.

The opportunity

Alison's extensive network contains many senior managers and executives, some of whom she placed many years ago and have remained loyal contacts since. Several have been in touch recently, seeking Alison's advice on adding non-executive directorships to their portfolio.

Alison realizes she can be 'the glue' in the market that unites company boards seeking fresh input with younger executives seeking their first non-executive directorship. Alison's thoughts turn to a coaching program that would make these younger executives more marketable and 'NED-ready'. Researching her database of contacts and the wider market, Alison discovers powerful evidence in favour of younger non-executive directors:

- The COVID-19 pandemic showed many leadership teams to be out of touch with new technologies and the dynamics of a younger, more mobile workforce.

- Younger board members offer fresh ideas and different thinking.

- Younger execs often want an NED alongside their current operational role. They bring more up-to-date experience than their older counterparts.

- Many have detailed knowledge of new technologies not currently known at board level.

Alison feels confident she can deal with the counter arguments against younger NEDs (such as potential conflicts of interest and the impact of the additional time commitment on family life).

Alison's head is buzzing, and she hurriedly jots down ideas while they're fresh in her mind:

- A program underpinned by coaching to help execs get their first NED. Working title: 'Your First NED' (YFN).

- Need three variants of YFN—Gold, Silver, and Bronze for different commitment levels/budgets.

- Once placed, keep the revenue stream going by selling the newly placed NED a support program that helps keep them organized and in control, given that they still have their full-time job and have just taken on a new part-time role with a totally different organization. Working title: NED Support Program (NSP).

- Maybe my existing presentation and comms training programs have a role to play?

- Maybe I can breathe new life into ExecUnet—the executive network club that didn't quite take off the way I hoped?

Alison opens P-CAM—and so should you. Carry on reading to see how Alison uses P-CAM to capture her ideas, expand them, and create a foundation for her approach to the new niche she's creating.

Record Your Perfect Client's Niche

Alison opens the **1-Niche** tab and enters rough notes about her perfect client into the light-grey cell.

> Exec (or member of leadership team) with operational responsibility. Open to their first NED role. Aged probably late-40 to late-50. No specific educational requirement, but probably >= degree level. Additional sector knowledge and participation a bonus, e.g. active membership of professional association

Grey cells are not processed by P-CAM, so you can enter as much information as you want.

In the light-blue input cell, Alison enters an abbreviated description of her perfect clients, capturing the essential elements.

> Young execs open to their first NED role

Notes on niches

Here are some additional notes on *niches* and *perfect clients* to help you start on the best footing. You might hear people talk about 'discovering' a niche in the same way miners might discover a seam of coal. This is unhelpful and misleading. Niches don't sit there waiting to be discovered by you (or your competitors).

Niches are *created*, not *discovered*. This can be a liberating concept—you have permission to 'create' a solution, as opposed to feeling that you have to 'hunt' for one. Alison used a combination of her sector knowledge and her imagination to come up with her 'young exec, first NED' niche, and you should do the same.

Don't be afraid to use a heavy dose of imagination: it's not all logic, knowledge, and measurement.

A final reminder on staying true to the perfect-client notion. It's tempting to wander into a description of people you *could* help. Stay the course and respond with your *perfect* client in mind: the client you would never tire of serving.

Capture Snapshots of Your Perfect Client's Life

The **2-Client** tab contains P-CAM's most complex tables, so you may need several visits to refine your ideas. Table 2a records nine categories of information, each of which I explain below using Alison's entries as examples.

Some people find it useful to have a specific person in mind when they are completing the tables—it helps keep them on track. You have the option of adding the Name and Job Title of an exemplar perfect client into the grey cells. Alison's entry is *Yusuf Aydin*, the *Vice President of Production at OutZing Engineering*. Yusuf is a close fit to the perfect client Alison has in mind for her new program. He is also a long-standing client and Alison feels comfortable sharing her thoughts on her new program and getting Yusuf's feedback.

Under the exemplar information—in the pale yellow cell—P-CAM has copied across from Table 1a your definition of the niche to which your exemplar client belongs. (You can see how Alison's entry has been copied across in your P-CAM download.)

The Exemplar column is a single reference point for the whole of the **2-Client** tab. In one place (on the left of Table 2a) you have the definition of your niche market and, as an additional reminder, the name of an exemplar perfect client.

Recording Core Desires and Pains

Table 2a allows you to record your perfect client's Core Desires and Core Pains. You can record up to seven of each, although

3–4 pairs should be enough. Take the time you need to feel really comfortable with your answers—they're the basis for products you'll define later.

Clearly, the more you understand your market and clients, the better you'll be able to complete these two columns. We all have loyal clients, and some of yours will most likely fit your definition of a perfect client. Tell them you're researching a new product and ask if you can interview them[19]. You'll be surprised at how willing people are to help. (Who doesn't enjoy talking about themselves?) You'll get some great input and the opportunity to recruit some beta testers for your new product/program.

We all have core desires, and you intuitively know what yours are. They should be what gets you out of bed in the morning. But what gets your perfect client out of bed in the morning? That's what you need to enter here.

Similarly, we all have core pains that hold us back from achieving our core desires. What are your perfect client's core pains? Can you match them against a core desire?

Your copy of P-CAM includes entities for four Core Desire/ Pain pairs, entered by Alison when she had Yusuf Aydin in mind. Here's a sample pair.

Core Desires: To give his kids what he didn't have (good education and lifestyle)

Core Pains: Fear of failure (letting his family down, not living up to his self-imposed expectations)

The next column along from Core Desires and Core Pains is Headline Solution. Time to see how Alison coped with that.

---

19 The Mom Test by Rob Fitzgerald is an excellent reference on speaking with clients regarding new products.

Identifying How Your Headline Solutions Help

You have a lot in common with Alison Tan. You both have a viable business that solves clients' problems. Alison looked at her perfect client's Core Desires and Pains and asked herself, "How can I reuse what I already have to help my new perfect client satisfy a core desire or neutralize a core pain?"

Keep that question in mind as you read through what Alison came up with, along with her thought process and ideas. (And remember, Alison Tan isn't real, and neither is her business. Her ideas don't have to be congruent or viable. Their purpose is to illustrate how P-CAM works.)

Alison Tan's Headline Solutions

Alison has a successful career in recruitment and a formal coaching qualification, with many happy clients in both camps. Alison studied the first desire/pain combination, summarized as:

Good education and lifestyle for family -V- Fear of failure

Considering everything she already had on the shelf, Alison felt confident that she could create a coaching-led program to address this, within the context of helping a perfect client secure their first non-executive directorship. She gave the program the working title 'Your First NED', knowing she'd fill in more details later, and completed the Headline Solution cell in Table 2a:

Coaching 1-2-1 (within YFN program)

Alison worked her way through the desire-and-pain pairings, all the while considering how she could use what she already had within the context of her new niche. The next:

Validation—make a difference -V- Feels 'passed over' / career plateaued

For this second pairing, Alison thought she could use her presentation and communications training as the basis for a product that helps her clients become more confident on stage and improve their professional and sector-specific profiles. She made a simple note to that effect and carried on.

The third desire-and-pain pairing caused Alison to stop and think.

Portfolio income ('insurance policy') -V- Feels stretched and stressed

Alison couldn't immediately think of an existing product she could adapt, but she understood the problem: a senior manager with a full-time job being worried about caving in when loaded up with an additional two or three part-time jobs for other organizations.

Alison came up with the idea of an 'NED Support Program', whose purpose was to do all the admin work associated with the NED roles and ensure the NED was fully briefed for each board meeting, etc. The more Alison thought about it, the more she warmed to the idea. She saw it as the next product she could sell to someone who had just secured their first NED role. It enhanced her revenue stream and kept her in touch with her most successful clients.

The final desire-and-pain pairing linked back somewhat to the earlier one about validation. Alison studied her earlier entry:

Bigger/broader professional network -V- Finds relationship building difficult

Alison had attempted to launch 'ExecUnet', a senior-level group program a couple of years back, but it hadn't got enough traction and eventually Alison had shelved the idea for another time. Maybe that time had arrived? She made a note to that effect in the Headline Solution column.

Group program (ExecUnet)

You need to be careful with your data entry in the Headline Solution column. P-CAM uses your input elsewhere, so it's vital that you're consistent. For example, P-CAM will view '1-2-1 Coaching' and '1-to-1 Coaching' as different solutions. (Entries are not case sensitive, so P-CAM will treat 'Online Course' and 'online course' as the same.)

Three Types of False Beliefs

We all doubt our ability occasionally; it's a natural part of our makeup. We've all had beliefs challenged as to why such-and-such won't work or so-and-so is no good. P-CAM allows you to record three categories of false belief: method, internal, and external.

A **false method belief** concerns how the solution is being delivered. You can liken it to a problem with the postal service rather than the parcel that's being delivered. For example, "I've tried online courses before, but the material has always been poorly structured and boring." The advice being offered by the courses might be fine. The problem lies with the method of delivery.

False internal beliefs are doubts people have with their own abilities. For example, "I'm too old to learn martial arts. I don't have the flexibility."

False external beliefs are problems people have with a third party. For example, "I've no time for [xxxx company]. They provide poor quality service."

Your job is to enter the false beliefs you believe your perfect client has with each of the headline solutions you just created. Your knowledge of these false beliefs comes from how well you know your clients and market. For example, what they might have let slip in meetings, comments you picked up at association conferences, or maybe surveys you conducted.

Here's what Alison entered relating to her YFN coaching program. You can read the complete set within P-CAM.

False Method Beliefs: Coaches want to know so much about you–takes forever, very inefficient

False Internal Beliefs: Questions whether he deserves his success ("I'll be found out one day")

False External Beliefs: Coaching is a flaky, unregulated market– how do you know the coach is any good?

Client Awareness

The final task to complete Table 2a is to assign your perfect client's awareness state for each headline solution. Use the drop-down menu to select one of four possible states:

- The client doesn't even recognize they have a problem

- The client knows they have a problem and can articulate it reasonably well

- The client has researched potential solutions (although may not know about mine)

- The client knows about my solution

You'll come across client awareness again in the next chapter and use it to create materials with a sharper focus.

Recording Your Client's Change in Status

Table 2b asks you to take a step back and describe your perfect client's life before and after your intervention—before and after they use your product, follow your program, or attend your workshop.

The table divides your client's before-and-after life into three categories: their overall situation, their average day, and their status. In total there are six input cells.

I believe this table is appropriate to most situations. Some of my colleagues and business pals didn't agree with me and couldn't see the value of this table. Here's a summary of their objections together with my response.

Will is an accountant by profession and a good pal of mine. He strongly believes the secret to the sale lies in showing the client how you can either 'make them money or save them money'. I disagree. The big bucks lie in changing your client's status. A Rolex watch, Hermès scarf, or Burberry overcoat all change the status of the wearer. A significant part of the elevated status feeling comes from the wearer feeling 'safe'. Who wouldn't trust Rolex, Hermès, or Burberry? How does what you deliver change their status?

"Those are all B2C examples", I hear you cry. "What about B2B?"

Same applies. Amazon Web Services (AWS) is the leading supplier of remote computing services. Most of the elite web-hosting services use AWS in some capacity. I host all my client websites on AWS and that elevates the status of the service I deliver to my clients. This gives them a feeling of security and in turn enhances their status. Their thinking is something like, *Active Presence is hosting my website on AWS. I really appreciate that they're looking after me. That helps me hold my head a little higher among my peers and clients. I don't just have any old website; I have one that's hosted on the best cloud platform.* This isn't new: a similar dynamic applied back in the 1980s, when IBM was the dominant IT supplier. IBM's customers—more correctly, the senior managers thereof—considered themselves a notch above their peers. IBM was never the cheapest solution, but it was highly trusted by its customers.

On reading an early copy of the manuscript, a colleague queried the applicability of Table 2b to 'more mundane' service businesses, such as a dog-walking service or oven-cleaning business. "Surely customers of such businesses aren't going to have a life-altering experience, so does the oven cleaner or dog walker really need to bother with this?" I believe they ought to, as it helps business owners differentiate between the 'perfect client' versus 'any old client'.

I have a client whose dog-related business started as a dog-walking service. Over the years she added dog-training classes and went on to write an incredibly successful book. I met her as she was creating a niche training product designed to fit the daily routine of busy new puppy owners. In summary, it comprises a step-by-step program that's delivered to the puppy owner's home each month. In the box is everything the new puppy owner needs to cover that month's training: toys, treats, instruction guide, links to supporting videos, etc. It's an exceptionally high-quality product that sells for a premium price. Jane developed her business way beyond dog walking by digging into the subjects in Table 2b, as they relate to the owners of new puppies:

Jane knows new-puppy owners seriously underestimate the time needed to look after and train their new pup. Most likely, prior to the pup arriving, the owner's 'average day' was already full. Dog-training classes are too far away and at the wrong time of day. The owner needs help they can access at their convenience. Having a well-behaved dog does more than make the owner happy. It changes the owner's self-perception, based on cues from neighbours and other dog owners, for example. Their puppy is friendly towards the neighbours' children, doesn't run around their gardens, or dig up the vegetable patch. Other dog owners comment how they wished they had such a well-behaved pet. People are willing to pay much more to hear nice things about themselves than they are to have their dog walked. Walking the dog is ticking a box on a to-do list; having a well-behaved family pet makes the owner feel good and changes how they perceive themselves (i.e. it changes their status).

Oven cleaning. A local pal of mine is a keen amateur chef: he loves his kitchen and cooking. He lives on his own in a big house and has converted part of it into a self-contained short-term let. The kitchen in the main house has two full-size ovens, plus a combination microwave oven. Adding in the separate studio, all the kitchen-cooking appliances comprise three ovens, two microwaves, two hobs, and two extractor fans—all of which need cleaning. My pal has high standards: he keeps the rental studio sparkling, so he can command high prices, and his own pride as a good chef drives his desire for a clean and tidy kitchen.

The local oven-cleaning company loves my pal; his single address generates as much cleaning revenue as three normal jobs. His kitchens are easier to clean, as the kitchen in the studio is hardly used and my pal's high standards means he has the ovens in the main house cleaned more frequently.

Is my pal the very definition of the oven cleaner's perfect client? 100%.

Does my pal know that and use it as leverage for a modest discount? Yes, and in recognition recommends the oven cleaner highly to other landlords. Both sides win. The oven cleaners get good, regular business and my pal's status for renting a sparkling clean holiday let—and being a cracking cook—are maintained.

While it's probably not possible to force fit every business into Table 2b, I hope these examples show how some deep thought about your perfect client and how you can impact their self-perception can generate worthwhile business opportunities.

Time to review Alison's entries.

Overall Situation (Before)

Alison describes her perfect client's life as:

> Perceived by colleagues and friends to have 'done well'—has a
> good job, with good rewards and a lot of responsibility.

The objective is to sketch a starting point. You can always come back and add more detail. Don't feel you have to get everything perfect in the first pass.

Overall Situation (After)

Following your intervention, what will your client's life look like? Here's Alison's entry:

> Busier, but less stressed. Has more than one income stream.
> Feels supported and better organized. Has spoken at industry
> conferences and been invited to another.

The contrast between the two situations allows Alison to see just how far her clients will have travelled—an important criterion overlooked by many clients and suppliers alike. Stephen Covey is fond of telling us all to 'start with the end in mind,' and this is one way of recording that, so you can track your progress and that of your clients.

Average Day (Before)

Use this cell to be more specific, refining an overall situation into an average day. Here's what Alison entered:

> Enjoys the professional parts of the job. Leaders call for his
> opinion, but only within the context of Production—not involved in
> wider leadership conversations, to which he feels he could make
> valid and useful contributions.

You can use this information in product design, as you look for areas where you can offer support and challenges you can help clients overcome.

Average Day (After)

Here's Alison's description of Yusuf's average day following working with Alison:

> Has delegated more professional tasks to team members and
> freed up 'head space' to think more about the wider sector and
> how his skills can be better utilized. Actively seeks participation
> in meetings where he could make a contribution and has been
> excluded (through innocent oversight).

Status (Before)

I've already commented on the importance of changing a client's status. Here's what Alison wrote about Yusuf:

> Feels under-appreciated and simultaneously a bit 'exploited'.
> Feels unfulfilled—wants to 'make an impact'.

What does your client's life look like?

Status (After)

Following her intervention, Alison describes Yusuf's status as:

> Much higher status. Recognized as being in a key leadership position both inside his company and externally. His opinion is sought by media covering their sector.

Perfect clients like Yusuf will pay a lot for such a change in their status. They see it as an investment in themselves, their future, and their self-worth.

Interpreting the Transformation Statements

Tab: 3-Transformation

You can find the transformation statements in Table 3a. P-CAM generates them based on what you've entered so far (in Tables 1a and 2a). Their purpose is to act as a reference point and help you create better product descriptions (which you'll be doing next). The statements don't have a life of their own outside of P-CAM, so don't be concerned if you find the style or grammar clunky.

Up to this point you've been using P-CAM to record information and thoughts about your perfect client. A brief reminder: defining your perfect client doesn't mean turning away business from those who aren't perfect clients. Clearly defining your perfect clients helps you more easily focus your marketing spend on them as a single group.

P-CAM creates the transformation statements according to this familiar model.

I help [who] achieve [goal] by overcoming [what]

The cell to the right of each transformation statement contains an 'awareness state' (also generated by P-CAM and based on your input).

Each transformation statement addresses a core desire/pain you identified in Table 2a. The data next to it shows how aware your client is of a solution. Here's an example from the data shipped with P-CAM.

I help [Young execs open to their first NED role] achieve [To give his kids what he didn't have (good education and lifestyle)] by overcoming [Fear of failure (letting his family down, not living up to his self-imposed expectations)]

The process up to now has forced you to think about your client base, define your perfect client and record their characteristics. You've thought about their beliefs and challenges, and how you might help them—at least in headline terms.

It's time to think more deeply about what you sell—your offers and associated products.

NUTSHELL NOTE #13

Nothing trumps knowing your perfect client better than they know themselves. Spend time working out how you could help them change their status.

12.

Using P-CAM to Create Product Definitions

Build something 100 people love,
not something 1 million people kind of like.

—Brian Chesky

Based on the thousands of websites my colleagues and I have analyzed in recent years, it's clear many owners of service businesses spend a lot of time and energy talking about their offer. I believe too few service businesses invest enough resources building clearly defined products based on that offer. For me, the end point is the product, not the offer. It's your product that clients purchase. It's your product that delivers the benefit your clients seek. It's product sales that deliver revenue to your business and generate profit.

My old maths teacher would have summarized it as, "Having an offer is a necessary but not a sufficient condition." A good offer, such as 'Best Fruit & Veg in the County' might get you a stall at the farmers' market, but you still need to stack your table with attractive, tasty fruit and vegetables if you want to make a sale.

Too few service businesses do this well. Far too many get woolly and fluffy the closer they get to their clients' bank accounts. You need tight, clear, specific product descriptions, and this chapter will show you how P-CAM can help you create them (based on the niche and client information you've already entered). Before launching into the details, I want to take a moment to iron out misconceptions surrounding offers and products.

People Buy Products, Not Offers

The difference between offers and products is fundamental, frequently confused, and has wide-ranging ramifications, so it's worth taking time to clarify the terms.

Seeking an example, I searched Google for 'accountants near me' and selected a website at random. The about-page contained the only information relating to the services the firm provided:

> Accountants based in [redacted] providing a wide range of services for individuals and businesses. With over 20 years experience our services include: Business Start ups; Business advice; Bookkeeping; VAT; Accounts preparation; Personal Tax Returns; Corporate Tax; Self Assessment; Payroll; Deputy Accounts.

With nothing else to draw me in—no specifics, no lead magnet, no detailed services page—it was a simple decision to click away and look elsewhere.

Another homepage proudly told me their firm was:

> The UK's top accountants for self-employed freelancers & consultants

Apart from clearly defining their target market, the homepage offered me a callback and promised I could 'get signed up in under 10 mins'. The firm told me they had nationwide coverage and offered an all-inclusive fee. All of this was in clear view 'above the fold', along with an offer of 'free business registration'. I wanted to know more. They clearly explained their fees on the 'Plans & Pricing' page and the 'What Our Clients Say' page was full to the brim with tons of social proof (Google reviews). If I wanted an accountant, this firm would certainly get a call from me. This second website converted me from a *visitor* to a *lead*, something the first website failed to do.

The first website was like many others we came across during our survey. It had no strong product focus. So what? Well, without a strong product focus, there's no real reason for visitors to stay. Websites like this fail to give visitors enough information to take the next step on the way to becoming a satisfied and loyal client. It's product sales that generate revenue, not empty marketing blurbs about 'client-centric partnerships', or 'going the extra mile'. Sites that don't have any product information are, quite literally, selling themselves short by not explaining how visitors could benefit.

Although the second website led with the bold claim of being, 'The UK's top accountants for self-employed freelancers & consultants', they had clearly priced, detailed product information to back it up. I could read what I would get as a client (and also read tons of social proof about how satisfied other clients are). What's not to like?

During our surveys, we reviewed many service businesses promoting programs (workshops, coaching, etc.) on a range of topics. Frequently these were described as being 'customized to the client's requirements'. While this may well have been true, it didn't give enough information to satisfy our curiosity. By not going one stage further and providing a lot more detail on specific programs, business owners were missing an opportunity to impress us (and Google: remember E-A-T.)

Attempting to be everything for everybody is a road to nowhere. As Brian Chesky, one of the co-founders of Airbnb, says in the quote that opens this chapter, "Build something 100 people love, not something 1 million people kind of like." Create a valuable offer for a niche market. Then satisfy the offer with products that solve pressing needs.

Following Brian Chesky's advice leads to the crunch point in the Website Effectiveness Framework—the point where many businesses get stuck. Progress through the tiers from Cogency to Systems Engagement and Community Engagement is natural enough. Consistent, diligent work tends to get rewarded. Not this time. The work is harder and needs to be coupled with a change in mindset.

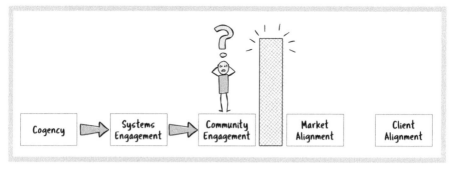

Figure 12-1: Poor product information prevents many website owners from progressing to Market Alignment, thereby reducing user engagement.

My experience is that website owners need a lot of help in making the leap to Market Alignment. An important concept is the purpose of primary, secondary, and tertiary offers and products. Getting to grips with this concept can have far-reaching consequences. From individual work with clients, I know many have to think more deeply about their businesses as they work through P-CAM. They end up viewing their products differently, sometimes repackaging elements to create new ones.

Primary, Secondary and Tertiary Offers and Products

Your **primary** product is (normally) the 'big-ticket' item in your catalogue—the highest revenue generator. Primary products represent a big payday for you and high value for your client. Most SME service businesses have low overheads, so their highest revenue products are normally the most profitable. This isn't always the case, in which case the primary product might not be the 'big-ticket' item, but the one generating the highest profit.

Consider your **secondary** product to be the one you sell when the client can't afford your primary product.

Your **tertiary** product is typically a trial product—a low-cost entry product a client could purchase to test whether they want a longer/deeper relationship with you.

Using Transformation Statements to Create Product Descriptions

P-CAM tabs 4, 5, and 6 address Offers and Products (O&P). There's a tab for each O&P category: primary, secondary, and tertiary. As the layout of all three tabs is identical, tab **4-O&P-Primary** serves as a good example for them all.

The transformation statements from tab 3 form the basis for all the tables in tabs 4-6. Here's a reminder of the format for the transformation statements:

I help [**who**] achieve [**goal**] by overcoming [**what**]

Creating Your Offer | Tab 4-O&P Primary

Table 4b pulls in data you entered earlier. When you recorded your perfect client's core pains, desires, etc. you also listed your 'Headline Solutions' (Table 2a).

Your headline solutions are now listed in a dropdown menu at the top of Table 4b. Open the dropdown and select the headline solution that's going to make your primary offering. (Use the same approach to select your secondary in Table 5b and your tertiary in Table 6b.) Looking at your P-CAM file, you can see Alison selected Coaching 1-2-1 (YFN Program).

In the remainder of Table 4b enter characteristics of the selected headline solution.

- Tangible deliverables

- What your headline solution makes

- What it saves

- How it increases your perfect client's status

Used together, this information defines your offer. Here are some of Alison's entries, as a worked example.

Tangible deliverables: List what you deliver to your clients— what's left behind after you've gone. Make each deliverable as tangible as possible. For each deliverable, ask yourself whether it creates something new for your client or whether it saves them something. (It might do both.)

For example, one of Alison's deliverables is an 'NED interview pack'.

What does it make? Here Alison enters what the NED interview pack creates: 'Delivers everything for a successful interview, e.g. updated c.v. and draft presentation, if appropriate.'

What does it save? You can think of this entry as how the client benefits. Alison enters how the NED interview pack benefits her client: 'Saves client's time in preparing and reduces chance of straying from plan.'

How does it increase your client's status? The previous chapter covered the importance of changing your client's status. The more you can show an increase in your client's status, the more they'll be willing to pay for your service.

Alison's entry of, 'Helps generate excellent first impression' would increase the client's status in the eyes of the interviewer and also improve the client's belief in themselves. This latter point is important, as status is as much an internal belief as it is the (external) belief of others.

Once you have this table complete (Table 4b) you have sufficient input to create a good homepage overview of your offer (in Alison's case, the 'Your First NED program'). The aim is to use the features and benefits to entice interested visitors to the product page for more detailed information.

Message Optimization | Table 4c

In Chapter 10, I described message optimization as tuning your message based on the awareness your client has of you and how you can help. These differences in awareness were first described by Eugene Schwartz in *Breakthrough Advertising*[20] way back in 1966. Schwartz defined five stages of awareness. Your perfect client will move through these stages in this order:

- **Problem unaware**: your client doesn't know they have a problem.

- **Problem aware**: your client recognizes they have a problem. They can explain it, but they don't know what the solution is.

- **Solution aware**: your client knows a solution exists and has actively researched the market, looking for the product that meets their needs.

20 Breakthrough Advertising is now back in print and available from https:// breakthroughadvertisingbook.com

- **Product aware**: your client has a product under consideration. They may still have some questions. They are looking for proof that their needs will be satisfied.

- **Most aware**: your client is almost ready to commit. By this stage you'll have a good relationship with your client and be able to supply any final encouragement that they might need.

From a marketing perspective, the first four stages are the most important. (Once a prospect is 'most aware,' closing the deal should be a sales formality.)

P-CAM generates content for Table 4c based on the solution you selected from the dropdown menu in Table 4a and the client's awareness you selected when completing Table 2a.

You'll recall, on the first page of this book—before the table of contents—I said if you wanted to be an excellent photographer, you had to be prepared to do the work: take lots of photos and critically examine the quality of your work.

Clients tell me they find this next section both eye-opening and hard work. If you want to truly serve your market, appeal to Google's E-A-T approach, and reap the rewards, then Table 4c is worth time and focus.

If you're using a professional copywriter, you should be able to rely on them for a thorough understanding of message tuning and client awareness. Of course, you'll still have to brief them, so you should at least be familiar with what's coming up in order to produce a good brief.

If you're writing your own copy, Table 4c gives you guidance on tuning your message. To save you cross-referencing P-CAM, I've repeated the guidance below and added examples.

Problem unaware

P-CAM guidance notes: No knowledge of the pain point or any potential solutions. Good ways to engage people in this group:

- Posts that provide background information. They need to be engagingly written (entertaining to read/view)
- Offer genuinely helpful information for free (useful giveaways)

Example

The results from the early Worldwide Digital Footprint surveys showed that many website owners did not understand the importance of HTTPS. Many failed to grasp that not upgrading from HTTP meant that browsers discriminated against their websites: they were truly 'problem unaware'. I wanted to help these website owners, but how do you help someone who doesn't even know they've got a problem?

At every opportunity, I talked, wrote, posted, and presented about the problem. I made an eight-minute educational video (plus a super-short InfoSnip that summarized the topic in under a minute) and publicized these as widely as possible[21]. I stayed true to Eugene Schwartz's model by explaining the background, making the videos as dynamic and engaging as I could, and offering genuinely helpful information for free.

It's likely your experience and expert knowledge allows you to see further than your clients and identify roadblocks they are yet to reach. What are those roadblocks? How can you ease your clients' journeys and win their trust? Think about topics you can talk about easily, with little preparation. This shouldn't be hard work. It didn't take me long to record an eight-minute video. From that one video, it was easy to create the shorter InfoSnip and use the video transcript as the foundation for blog posts, emails, etc.

21 Both the video and InfoSnip can be found on my YouTube channel.
Video – https://youtu.be/2dHDWwA_VGU
InfoSnip – https://youtu.be/z2TvCe1oExl

Problem aware

P-CAM guidance notes: Know they have a problem, but that's all. (They don't yet know anything about any potential solutions.) Good ways of engaging people in this group:

- Offer empathy
- Make it clear that you understand their experience
- Offer potential solutions (several thereof)

Example

Many owners of SME businesses struggle with their websites but can't quite put their finger on the issue. They have a nagging feeling they aren't getting their money's worth. They're aware they have a problem, but many aren't really sure what it is or how or fix it. I created the Website Effectiveness Framework to help website owners understand the confusion of rapidly changing website technologies.

I popularized WEF through the same channels I used for messages about HTTPS (and other issues). However, this time I came with a potential solution, instead of loading yet another problem onto the desks of time-poor business owners.

By conducting studies for five years prior to creating WEF, and combining the results with my career experience, I was confident I understood the struggles business owners had with their websites. I referred to the survey findings to give website owners some comfort: they weren't alone in finding many aspects of website ownership confusing or contradictory.

Can you do something similar for your market? Something for those would-be perfect clients of yours—the ones who know they have a problem but don't yet know enough to picture a solution? Experiment by starting small. For example, prior to investing a ton of time and effort in creating the Website Effectiveness Framework, I created the 'Website 5 Star Review'. This was a simple online survey. It took less than a minute to complete and gave the user a simple five-star rating for their website. It was a great way to help website owners and simultaneously test the market. What could you do for your perfect clients?

Solution aware

P-CAM guidance notes: Know that a solution to their problem exists but don't know the specific product that provides it. Good ways of communicating with people in this group:

- Provide education—be helpful
- Describe the alternative approaches/solutions available. Look for a way to distinguish yourself from other suppliers

Example

Building on the Website Effectiveness Framework, the next logical step was to help website owners prioritize their development effort. The response from early adopters of the framework was, "I get how this framework clarifies the general problem, but how does it help me deal with the crock of crap I have right now?" Website owners were making semi-educated guesses as to how they ought to spend their website budget, as already discussed in earlier chapters.

The Website Effectiveness Assessment gave website owners a way to benchmark their site against the framework. It helped them decide which bit of their crock to focus on first. To preserve my position of being objective and helpful, I made the WEA freely available and didn't link it to any services sold by my company, Active Presence.

The combination of the assessment and framework is unique in the range of business owners it helps. It can help those with limited IT knowledge audit a website they don't really understand. It can also help IT-savvy website owners spend their budgets on the right thing at the right time.

There are people out there who are the perfect client for you. They're looking around the market right now, having done a pile of research. If they don't know about you yet, what can you offer the market that would boost your popularity while allowing you to demonstrate your expertise? If they know about you, offer shedloads of proof that you can meet their needs (see next).

Product aware

P-CAM guidance notes: Know about your product but aren't yet convinced that it's for them. A vital aspect of communicating with people in this group is addressing their objections. Deal with all their reasons as to why your product might not be right for them.

The next stage is to take them into some form of product trial. This is normally signalled by people asking what your "offer is", or how the "deal is structured", etc. Two important points in responding to these signals are:

- Make a trial as easy as possible to implement
- Make it as risk free as possible (easy to reverse, no money or commitment required, etc.)

Example

Product trials are reasonably easy for software vendors to organize. It's harder if your product depends more on your personal input (for example, coaching, psychological services, accounting, legal services). Where 'you' are a large part of the solution, your prospective client will have two primary concerns: can this person do the job, and will I be able to work with them?

Client testimonials and detailed case studies can help answer the first question. The answer to the second comes down to the chemistry between you and your client. In the creative environment it's common for agencies and prospective clients to hold 'chemistry meetings'. These last between 30–50 minutes and are conducted for no fee. The purpose is to establish whether you can work together, rather than demonstrate/assess capabilities. The client will want to feel comfortable that their needs are going to be met.

The supplier will want to feel that their new client is reliable, will turn up for meetings on time and deliver their contributions to the project according to plan.

Recording Product Description Content | Table 4d

Use Table 4d to record content that will make its way into your final product description. You may be tempted to skip this step and write your website copy directly, based on Table 4b. The intermediate step of completing Table 4d provides an insurance policy—it ensures you don't forget anything and captures important details in one central point for future reference.

The subheadings below match those in Table 4d. Under each, you'll find an explanation, followed by the content Alison entered (based on her 'Your First NED' program).

Product name

Good product names capture the essence of what the product does while simultaneously creating some intrigue. Your products might be individual or exist as part of family. The rule of three[22] works well for naming products, especially within a family. For example, we used this principle at Active Presence for the website series of products:

- Website Effectiveness Framework

- Website Effectiveness Assessment

- Website Value Scan

- Website Content Engager

22 A writing principle that suggests a trio is more memorable than other number groupings. See Wikipedia, https://en.wikipedia.org/wiki/Rule_of_three_(writing)

Each name gives you a notion as to what it does, and if that captures your interest, it's likely that you'll scan the tag line for more information (coming next).

Made-up words or acronyms that can be pronounced as a word also work well, provided they convey something about what the product does.

- I created InfoSnip from 'information' and 'snippet'. We describe them as 'super-short video summaries of information that [insert your target market] ought to know' We have a library of our own and also create them for clients.

- The Product-Client Alignment Matrix is a bit of a mouthful but works quite well when the acronym is pronounced as a word, 'pea-cam'.

Alison's entry

'Your First NED' (aka YFN program)

Capture whatever ideas you have in P-CAM. You might think you'll remember them, but I guarantee you won't. And separate scraps of paper either get lost or misfiled. Don't worry about getting it perfect. Creativity is an iterative process.

Tagline

My experience of writing taglines is that they're like buses: you wait for ages, and then a bunch appear all at once. Capture them all, as you may end up using some somewhere else later on. Taglines tell the visitor whether they're in the right place. For example, the tagline under the logo on my Chris Davidson website is:

Websites & tools for service-oriented businesses

I came up with something similar to this when I was thinking about a tagline for the website family of products. However, I realized it made more sense to use it as a tagline for the entire site.

Taglines should add understanding (rather be an advertising slogan). In the world of business books, subtitles do the job of tag lines. For example:

- *Deep Work: Rules for Focused Success in a Distracted World* by Cal Newport

- *The Mom Test: How to Talk to Customers and Learn If Your Business Is a Good Idea When Everyone Is Lying to You* by Rob Fitzpatrick

- *Obviously Awesome: How to Nail Product Positioning so Customers Get It. Buy it. Love it.* by April Dunford

The titles (product names) are short and capture attention. The subtitles (taglines) answer, "Might this be useful to me? Do I want to know more?"

Alison's entries

Your First NED: Get the help that lands the role
Be first past the post with Your First NED

It's always worth having spare taglines, so don't procrastinate in the search for perfection. Capture ideas. Move on.

Who is it for?

You should be able to lift this from the niche table (Table 1a).

Alison's entry

Execs (or members of leadership teams) preferably with operational responsibility. They should be open to, or actively seeking their first

> NED. Probably aged 48 to 57. No specific educational requirement, but probably >= degree level. Additional sector knowledge and participation a bonus, e.g. active membership of professional association, good sector contacts, speaks at sector conferences, etc.

Where would it be used?

Deal with practical issues that might get in the way of your client using your product.

For example, in what languages is your product available? At Active Presence we have clients who work in multiple languages and for whom we've created multilingual websites. (You can read about two of them in the case studies.) If you operate in different languages or time zones, how do you support all your clients? Are there professional or legal restrictions on where you can offer your services? (For example, British solicitors need to bear in mind that Scottish law differs from English and Welsh law.)

Alison's entry

> YFN is for the UK market, i.e. UK organizations seeking Non-Execs. Candidates don't have to be UK nationals, but would clearly need to have a good understanding of the UK business and social environments. YFN is also appropriate to public sector bodies (e.g. NHS, education, local government) and third sector (charity, social enterprise).

When would it be used?

Give background on how your product helps clients overcome the core pains highlighted in Table 2a. This is a great opportunity for you to build trust based on your expert knowledge.

Alison's entry

> The COVID pandemic took its toll on many organizations, a lot of whom shed staff. Many pre-COVID posts declared redundant,

but also people leaving voluntarily, as part of the 'great shake up' triggered by the pandemic.

Businesses have been reinvented as old business models are declared no longer fit for purpose. Technology has come to play a greater role.

YFN helps organizations broaden their boards and deliver more skill to their boards, so they can make better decisions in face of all these huge changes.

What are the product's basic details?

This is based on the offers in Table 4b. Explain your product details—the tangible deliverables, etc. This section gives a very practical answer to the question, "What am I buying?"

This section can get quite involved, so when it comes to website layout, the designer will need to come up with an outline that prevents the reader from getting bogged down. Hint: concertina FAQ lists can be useful. They allow visitors to see a list of questions and open individual questions to read the answer.

Alison's entry

The program is underpinned by 1-2-1 coaching, with several add-on elements particular to helping candidates get their first non-exec directorship.

- 10 hours of coaching, split over 6 sessions
- Telephone/Zoom support as required (see further below)
- By (approx) midway through coaching would expect to have 'Your First NED' project plan completed
- We create for a draft of presentation for use during interviews
- We seek out suitable NED roles for clients
- For each role we prepare a file containing company info (including current board structure) and what the organization is looking for in the NED they seek
- For each role we create customized c.v. our client can use

- For each interview we create an interview plan, complete with likely questions
- For each interview we hold a mock interview (by Zoom) to test the plan

Why is it better than your competitors?

Entries here should be based on Table 4b and your marketplace knowledge.

Alison's entry

Summary of benefits

- Our clients are better prepared—they make a better first impression, increases chances of being successful (evidence: plan, customized c.v., mock interviews, draft presentations). We've known our clients for many years, tracked their careers and are more likely to be able to select NED roles suitable to their skills
- We save our client's time—we only put someone forward if we believe they would be a good fit and then we work hard with them for their success. It's a time-efficient process
- Even if unsuccessful, our clients are recognized as being credible and competent, which (i) increases their chances next time around and (ii) helps expand their network (as many companies will reach out to 'top-flight' unsuccessful candidates to have them in their orbit for future opportunities)
- Our ability to get the interviews because of our extensive connections with organizations—the benefit is that it's very efficient from client's POV—saves their time

How does the product work

You want to write about features and processes here. Describe what happens after someone buys your product. What journey do you take them on?

Alison's entry

1. Clarify client's needs/expectations w.r.t. NED role. (This is their first NED and we want to make sure we're all on their first page.)

2. We start looking for NED roles that would fit our client's skills. In particular we approach organizations that might not be formally advertising but where we feel the fit might be exceptional

3. (Conducted in parallel with step 1) We start the 1-2-1 coaching (based on step 1). If the client is a long-standing one, then initial progress will be more rapid, based on our prior knowledge of one another.

4. (During step 3) We jointly complete the NED Project Plan, taking account of the client's skills, aspirations, type of role, etc.

5. When we've made enough progress with understanding skills and roles, we'll start looking for advertised NED opportunities.

6. (Repeated each time a client is called for interview) We prepare a detailed background file on the organization and opportunity, including a draft presentation (if required) and potential questions the client might want to ask.

7. (Repeated each time a client is called for interview) We conduct mock interviews to help the client prepare well. (Although our clients are experienced execs, it will most likely be many years since they have formally interviewed, and all their previous interviews will have been for operational roles—not an NED role—we focus on that difference during the mock interviews.)

Key Performance Indicators (KPI)

The client should be able to measure these as part of the process of building trust and accountability. They should be based on Table 4b.

Alison's entry

1. We guarantee 2 interviews per quarter (measured from point at which role aspirations identified and client interview ready)
2. If the client is not offered at least 1 x NED within 12 months of us actively seeking directorships for that client, then we will return 50% of the first year's fee.
3. We will be available for all scheduled meeting (i.e. clients of this program are our top priority, so meetings only cancelled in unavoidable circumstances (accident/illness, etc.))
4. We will turn round c.v. edits within 48 hours
5. Pre-interview packs will be with the client at least 7 working days before interview
6. Whenever possible, mock interviews will be conducted at least 4 working days prior to the interview (sometimes not possible when short-notice interview opportunities arise)

Testimonials

We all know the value of social proof, so don't forget to include it, or ask for it in the first place. Collect both qualitative and quantitative testimonials. Include photos where possible, along with full names.

The Final Product Description

You have all you need to create a cracking product description. You can do this yourself or use P-CAM to brief a copywriter.

To illustrate the power of P-CAM as a briefing tool, I asked a copywriter to produce the product description below. As input, I provided the copy of P-CAM you've downloaded, along with the introduction to Alison's business from the beginning of Chapter 11. Here's the copywriter's first draft, word for word.

> This program is designed for professionals who want to make an impact and raise their status in the process. Ultimately, they want to become recognized as leaders within their company and in

their industry as well. Their authority will attract media attention and their opinion will be sought on important topics. Taking on a NED role is an investment in themselves and their career.

How we help:
Our clients achieve success more easily because they make a strong first impression. The careful planning we do together, combined with a customized CV, rounds of mock interviews, and draft presentations, prepares them well and sets them apart from their competitors. Clients also benefit because we have known them for many years, tracked their careers, and we can select NED roles suitable to their skills.

We save our clients valuable time when we secure interviews for them, thanks to our extensive connections with organizations. And we only put someone forward if we believe they will be a good fit and then we work hard with them for their success. No matter what, our clients increase their chances next time around because they're seen as being credible and competent. They also expand their network as many companies will reach out to 'top-flight' candidates who almost made the cut and keep them in mind for future opportunities.

Our process is straightforward:
First, we clarify our client's needs/expectations about an NED role and begin one-to-one coaching. Then we look for NED roles that best fit our client's skills. In particular, we approach organizations that may not advertise a role, but where we feel the fit might be exceptional. While we look, we jointly complete the NED Project Plan, taking account of the client's skills, aspirations, and desired role.

Each time a Your First NED client is called for an interview, we prepare a detailed background file on the organization and opportunity, including a draft presentation (if required) and potential questions the client might want to ask. And we conduct

143

mock interviews to help the client prepare well, especially if it's been several years since they have been interviewed.

Here's our guarantee:
- Identify our client's aspirations for a NED role and secure two interviews per quarter and prepare the client for the interviews.
- If the client is not offered at least one NED within 12 months of us actively seeking directorships for that client, then we will return 50% of the first year's fee.
- We will be available for all scheduled meetings.
- We will turn around CV edits within 48 hours.
- Pre-interview packs will be with the client at least seven working days before an interview.
- Whenever possible, mock interviews will be conducted at least four working days prior to the interview.

This program succeeds for clients because of the one-to-one coaching, the phone or Zoom support as needed, the interview preparation, and the professional connections we utilize to match clients with ideal organizations.

Your First NED is an ideal program for young executives seeking their first NED role. Many are perceived as having done well, yet they recognize they need help with placement for an NED role. We prepare them in every way and help them make it a reality while saving them time and frustration along the way.

In a condensed 540 words, the copywriter communicated the essential points: a description of the process, a summary of the benefits, and an outline of the guarantees. A separate table of features, plus a call-to-action would complete the website page.

You've now seen P-CAM used from start to finish. The copywriter produced such a good first draft not just because she's a talented writer, but because she was also working from a clear, tight brief. In her email to me, she said, "You are demonstrating the effectiveness of the P-CAM process right here—because you prepared me well and I knew what to write, it was written effectively."

The same approach would create product descriptions for the secondary and tertiary products.

NUTSHELL NOTE #14

Too few businesses do a good job of focusing their products on the needs of their perfect clients. Clearly communicate your process, benefits, and guarantees, and you'll have an immediate advantage.

Part F

Client Alignment (WEF Tier 5)

13.

Move the Goalposts and Radically Change Your Business

Don't wait for the right opportunity: create it.

—George Bernard Shaw

If you followed the early guidance, you will have arrived at this chapter by one of two routes. Those wanting to improve the performance of an existing website will have read all the previous chapters in sequence. Those with a bright idea but no website, will have jumped here from the end of Part B.

Readers with an existing website: If you've got this far and diligently applied the content, then your business and website should be in pretty good shape.

Tier 1 has left you with a well-performing website that Google treats favourably in its search returns.

Tiers 2 and 3 have given you a system for driving traffic to your website, where visitors find helpful, engaging content. You offer some high-quality free help to encourage those that could be a good fit for what you do to sign up and start an online relationship with you.

Tier 4 has helped you create a sharp focus on your perfect client and clarify your product definitions so they better meet market needs.

Surely that's it? Job done. Relax and enjoy the fruits of your labour. You can do this, and many companies do. Tier 5, Client Alignment, takes things a step further. Tier 5 is for people who want to rewrite the rule book and apply their expertise to creating a new normal that causes a permanent change in the market.

Readers with an idea and no website: This will help you crystalize your thoughts before reading Part E and using P-CAM to create content. Studying Part D will then help you find and engage your perfect potential clients. When you're ready to build your website, reviewing Part C will help you ensure all the technical foundations are in place.

Before looking more closely at how rule books get rewritten and deciding whether it's a path you want to follow, here are some examples.

The Aircraft that Rewrote the Rule Book

Geoffrey de Havilland was the British aircraft designer whose company (the de Havilland Aircraft Company Limited) created the Mosquito during World War Two. It was a revolutionary aircraft in several ways and so successful it triggered a permanent change in the conduct of aerial warfare. Without getting too bloody about it, prior to the 'Mossie', heavily armed, four-engine bombers with big crews made up the backbone of air force bomber fleets worldwide. History provides an almost endless record of such aircraft: the Avro Lancaster, Boeing B-17 Flying Fortress, Consolidated B-24 Liberator, Handley Page Halifax, Short Sterling, Boeing B-29 Superfortress. The list goes on.

Then along came the Mosquito, which had two engines, not four, and a crew of two, not somewhere closer to a dozen. It could fly faster and further—and with a heavier bomb load—than many of the traditionally designed aircraft. To cap it all, the Mosquito had zero defensive armament, relying on its speed to evade enemy aircraft.

It wasn't just the aircraft's performance that was game changing. You could look at the Mosquito from many points of view and still come away with evidence of de Havilland's brilliance. For example, he specified the fuselage and wings were to be made of wood. This gave a smooth, rivet-free finish that contributed to the Mosquito's high top speed. Metals were in short supply during the war, whereas wood was plentiful. De Havilland's design wasn't competing with other manufacturers for scarce resources. Metal workers too were in short supply; they were predominantly young men and had been drafted into the armed services at the outbreak of hostilities. However, there were plenty of older woodworkers available, who were too old for military service. The UK also had plenty of furniture manufacturers used to working in wood. When viewed from the perspective of having to manufacture the aircraft using the UK's limited resources, the Mosquito was also a game changer.

The story shows how well Geoffrey de Havilland understood the problem and his client (the Air Ministry). He had the answer to what the Ministry believed was an insoluble problem: a high-performance aircraft that could be built using non-strategic resources. The Ministry so firmly believed the problem was insoluble that, initially, they were highly skeptical of de Havilland's proposals. One Air Ministry official secretly supported de Havilland, and together they got the prototype airborne. Once flying, the proof was there for all to see. De Havilland created a new normal. The Mosquito changed the design of all aircraft that flew in its wake.

Many smaller organizations may feel overwhelmed by the enormous scale of the Mosquito story. We're not all made like Geoffrey de Havilland, and many of us don't employ thousands of staff working across multiple factories. But you don't have to think like de Havilland to change the world, and nor—thankfully—do you need to be involved in a war. You can apply your skill and expertise at a microscopic level and still have an enormous impact, as my father proved over sixty-five years ago.

Using Professional Skill to Create a New Normal

Dad was an ear, nose, and throat (ENT) surgeon who pioneered a surgical approach to the jaw joint. His paper, *Endaural Condylectomy* was published in the *British Journal of Plastic Surgery* in 1955[23]. In the paper, Dad explains how colleagues in facial reconstruction approached him for help, having run out of their own ideas for helping one of their patients. The surgeons pooled their skills and experience and carefully drew up a plan that delivered an immense improvement in the patient's quality of life.

The benefits extended far beyond that one patient. The publishing of Dad's paper popularized his approach and brought about a permanent, wide-scale change in a previously established surgical procedure. This marked a step change that created a new normal and a better outcome for all patients from that point onwards.

Can You Create a New Normal?

Can you create a permanent shift in your market by creating a new normal—a new way of solving an issue that deeply affects your niche? To do so, you need to have solid, detailed answers to these two questions:

1. Do you know your client better than they know themselves?
2. Can you prove it?

Compare Dad with Geoffrey de Havilland. The latter understood the Air Ministry's problem better than they understood it themselves—and went on to prove it. By solving the Air Ministry's seemingly insoluble problem, de Havilland succeeded where all

---

23 Endaural Condylectomy, A S Davidson FRCS DLO, https://www.jprasurg.com/article/S0007-1226(55)80013-6/pdf

other aircraft manufacturers had failed. It was the previous failure of the many that created the mystical 'belief' that it was impossible to build a high-performance aircraft from non-strategic resources.

By the time of the operation, Dad and the rest of the surgical team knew their patient better than she knew herself (at least regarding her temporo-mandibular joint). Over sixty-five years later, Dad's paper is still cited. In pioneering a fresh approach to the temporo-mandibular joint, Dad created a new normal. He changed his part of the world for the better.

George Bernard Shaw held controversial views, but his comment at the start of the chapter about creating an opportunity rather than waiting for it to arrive is bang on the money. I know some business owners miss this point because I overhear them talking about, 'discovering such-and-such a niche'.

GBS gives you the answer and although mentioned earlier, it bears repeating: you don't discover a niche, you create it. And you create it at the intersection of *what you know* and *what your market needs*.

I was driven to action after hearing one-too-many tales of woe from small-business owners who'd handed over more cash than they needed to and ended up with a rat's nest of marginally capable IT. This book is my attempt to fix that injustice. In researching it, I discovered the problem is far from one-sided. Business owners tend not to invest in their education, and the majority don't know enough about managing IT projects or IT suppliers.

Another tranche of issues lies with tech-savvy youngsters who don't have enough business experience. The IT sector is losing valuable skill as people my age—who were there at the beginning—retire and take up gardening or fly fishing. Not enough skills transfer is taking place. I'd consider it a great success if the Website Effectiveness Framework became the standard for improved conversation between IT suppliers and clients. That's why I sat down at my desk and started pecking at my keyboard.

Is the Light Worth the Candle?

In deciding whether you want to attempt to create a new normal, there's an important point to make: you can have a very successful business from within the Market Alignment tier without the struggle of getting into Client Alignment. And it is a struggle. You'll need a strong passion to give you the energy to overcome the obstacles that will be in your way. De Havilland was driven by desperate times and exceptional national need. Dad was a dedicated surgeon who saw a way to radically improve the quality of life for a patient who had run out of options—and create a way forward for others in a similar position. Assuming you have that overriding passion to fuel your way, here are other considerations.

Don't expect to be thanked

Geoffrey de Havilland's revolutionary design put a lot of noses out of joint. To help the Allied war effort, he made all his design work and drawings freely available to Allied aircraft manufacturers. Here's what the American Beech Aircraft company had to say about the Mosquito:

> *"This airplane has sacrificed serviceability, structural strength, ease of construction, and flying characteristics in an attempt to use construction material that is not suitable for the manufacture of efficient airplanes."*

As recorded earlier, the British Air Ministry was also skeptical. The Minister of Aircraft Production, Lord Beaverbrook, reportedly told Air Vice-Marshall Freeman to halt the development of the Mosquito. Thankfully, Freeman never received a direct written order to that effect and ignored the Minister. The successful progression of the project owes a lot to the support of one person. The Mosquito was as much Freeman's success as it was de Havilland's.

A good idea isn't always recognized as such. You may end up ahead of the market. If you do, you need to accept that a large part of your early work will be educating your market before they will consider buying from you. This has a direct impact on your website content and layout. For example, my decision to write this book led me to rebuild my entire website. Of course, there's a webpage about the book, but it goes beyond that. The homepage header image replays the book's subtitle. There's new homepage content about the book, and the Website Effectiveness Assessment plays a central role. I need to do all this because my target market doesn't know what the Website Effectiveness Framework is. And until they do, I'm limited in my ability to help them.

De Havilland didn't need to take such an educational approach with his detractors. Once the Mosquito was flying, its performance overcame all objections.

You only need one believer to start a movement

The flip side of having to struggle against all the doubters and naysayers is that you only need one believer to start a movement. One stone can make a lot of ripples. One client can prove your approach.

Adopt a collaborative approach with that first client. Be prepared to work together to solve the big challenge that you see the market struggling with, as de Havilland did with Air Vice-Marshall Freeman. No matter how much research you've done, there's a good chance that unexpected issues will appear. Be prepared to ditch your initial plan in favour of new realities. Keep your work real and focused on the big issue. Solve it for one. Document it well. Repeat for another. Adjust and repeat a few times until you're really confident. And then promote it like mad by applying the other four tiers of the Website Effectiveness Framework.

Your one lead client will be a loyal supporter. You solved an immense problem for them. Ensure you collect lots of case study and testimonial material for use on your website and associated social media.

Success lies in preparation

Dad was fond of the Army maxim 'time spent in reconnaissance is seldom wasted'. He's quite right. Don't go off half-cocked. Once you have your believer on board, spend time with them testing the critical points of your thesis. Don't shy away from using multiple minimum viable products (MVP) to do this. Successive small iterations will work out quicker and cheaper than going all-out and getting it wrong.

As an example, for the first round of market research I undertook for 'website effectiveness' I restricted the survey population to 500 websites, enough to judge whether I was onto something. With the comfort of a positive result, I expanded future surveys. The 2021 Digital Footprint Survey analyzed over 1,800 websites worldwide. I've underpinned this book with five annual studies, client projects, and a career in IT. I'm pretty sure I'm on the right track.

NUTSHELL NOTE #15

Create a commanding market position by producing a permanent market change for a niche you created.

You've made it to the end. Nearly. Coming up, are case studies that explain how my colleagues and I have applied the concepts you've just read about. There are also additional notes from me, plus an invitation to get involved in the next book, which is already well underway.

I practice Goju Ryu karate, and we have seven words that keep us going when the going gets tough: practice daily, be courageous, never give up.

Part G

Case Studies

14.

Frank Rogers
Law

Within the first six months of working with Chris Davidson, I was on 'Page 1' for some key search terms and since then massive progress has been made. The statistics are way beyond my expectations. Chris has an excellent team and his communications are clear and consistent. My business growth is due to his outstanding work.

—Frank Rogers

WEBSITE SEO

How we put Frank Rogers' website at the top of Google and triggered an enormous increase in enquiries.

Case-Study Scope

This case study illustrates work within the Cogency, Community and Systems Engagement, and Market Alignment tiers of the Website Effectiveness Framework. The Market Alignment work is a good example of how an SEO specialist can work with a website designer to create more traffic and business.

https://frankrogerslaw.co.uk

Frank Rogers Law

Frank Rogers is a UK-based solicitor who specializes in driving-related offences. Frank established his practice towards the end of 2020, following a long and distinguished career in partnership positions with other law firms. Frank developed his practice based on the network of contacts he'd developed over his long career, plus his exceptional reputation. Although a great way to kickstart his new practice, Frank was keen to generate more business via his website, especially considering how quickly the world adopted video meetings when COVID-19 reshaped the workplace.

When Frank approached me for help, I decided to start with an SEO audit of his website. As the site was new it didn't have much content, and I was confident we could accomplish the audit quickly and suggest a way forward.

Although SEO has become more intricate over time, the foundations underpinning the work remain unaltered.

You want **pillar content** to form the backbone of your site. This should be solid, reliable, and detailed content that addresses needs that many of your clients will have at some point. You can be sure that this content will be well visited. It will attract the right type of traffic and will be noticed by Google. Our SEO audit unearthed some great opportunities for creating new pillar content.

Internal links are an aspect of on-site optimization that are frequently overlooked. As the name suggests, they are links between pages and are a good way to provide additional SEO support to key pages. Clearly, the more content you have, the greater the opportunity for internal links.

Our first task for Frank was to create the pillar content to start generating more website traffic. Once we had more traffic to the website, we could start redirecting it via internal links.

Backlinks remain an important part of all good SEO strategies. We started a backlink strategy in parallel with producing the pillar content. This helped drive more traffic to the site and improved the site's overall rankings, as the backlinks were from domains with high Domain Authority[24].

Aside from optimizing the website, we also created a Google My Business profile for Frank Rogers Law and ensured it was updated regularly with fresh content and client reviews. The profile generates direct phone calls to Frank's office, in addition to pushing more traffic through to his website.

Results

We compared the monthly pageviews and new sessions for the month we started working with Frank to the situation a year later. Monthly pageviews had increased by sixteen times and the number of new sessions per month by twenty-six times. The office receives double-digit phone calls per month. The site was on the first page of Google for three of Frank's target keywords.

When informed by a well-managed SEO strategy, content creation coupled with detailed site changes can yield good results over the long term. SEO is not a quick fix, but it performs well when integrated with your business strategy.

WEF Alignment

Comparing the project with the Website Effectiveness Framework illustrates how the framework can be used as a benchmark, to check essential points are addressed.

Cogency

The website was created after July 2019 and therefore would automatically be subject to Google's mobile-first indexing policy.

---

24 Domain Authority (DA) is a search engine ranking score developed by Moz. See: https://moz.com/learn/seo/domain-authority

The site uses HTTPS, renders well on mobile devices and loads quickly.

We regularly monitor the website traffic and over time were surprised to discover nearly 70% of the website visitors use mobile phones. This is a far higher percentage than all my other clients and shows the importance of delivering a good service on all devices.

There are always opportunities for detailed adjustments, metadata being a good example.

Systems and Community Engagement

Frank Rogers has excellent Community Engagement going back many years. He's been deeply involved with the local Chamber of Commerce and Law Society, and maintains an active LinkedIn profile. He's well known in local business circles. This gave Frank an excellent springboard from which to launch his new business.

From a systems perspective we made some interesting observations. The search engine optimized blogposts attract a large readership. Ranking them against the homepage, and using pageviews or unique pageviews as a metric, produces interesting results. Typically the homepage is in position 5–6, with the leading positions being popular blogposts. This is backed up by visitor journey analysis that shows blogposts are the most common landing pages. Visitors move from the blog to other pages, discovering more about the firm's services as they do so. This illustrates the success of the ongoing SEO work.

Market and Client Alignment

The firm has a simple and effective alignment strategy, and this informed the site architecture. Services are aligned to the clients' needs by focusing on common driving offences. Clients approach the firm wanting help with such-and-such an offence and can easily find the service they need.

15.

Team ANDARE

Chris Davidson's innovative, solid, and reliable approach has given us a more visible, reliable, and flexible website. The website radiates who we want to be and how we want to position ourselves—and Chris has been very supportive in helping us through that process.

—Paul ter Wal, Founder and CEO, Team ANDARE

LAYOUT OF NEW PRODUCTS, PLUS LEAD-MAGNET CREATION

Example of deciding how to present new products, plus introducing a new assessment-based lead magnet.

Case-Study Scope

Read this case study to see how we went about laying out new products within the overall website design. The project is a good illustration of work in the Market Alignment tier, showing how we used P-CAM to create new products and their descriptions. We also did some work in the Systems Engagement tier: you can also read about how we went about creating a new assessment-based lead magnet.

https://team-andare.com and https://team-andare.nl

Team ANDARE

Paul ter Wal founded Team ANDARE to help organizations increase effectiveness by improving staff engagement and accountability. The company operates internationally from its base in The Netherlands, a country whose population is renowned for its multilingual abilities. This led us to creating websites in Dutch, English, and Italian.

Paul has a former career as a lawyer specializing in employment law. Initially, Team ANDARE helped its clients by focusing on the legal aspects of their relationships with their employees—for example, improving employee engagement by reassessing employment contracts and reducing sick leave. Paul wanted a broader scope for his firm. He wanted to help client organizations in ways that went beyond their employment contracts with their employees. This is a complex area, and although Paul and his team knew a lot and were trusted by their clients, the broader scope lacked specificity. This led to uncertainty in the team and potential confusion with clients.

Paul approached us for help in clarifying Team ANDARE's revised offer and product range, taking the broader scope into account. We worked our way through P-CAM, applying the method described in Chapters 11 and 12.

An issue Paul brought to the table was clients wanting to 'run before they could walk'. Many wanted to improve employee engagement but without taking the intermediate steps. We identified three distinct products and laid them out on the website in a very clear running order, numbered 1, 2, and 3.

The numerical sequence of the programs gave us the opportunity to create a 'Step 0' program, which was a free lead magnet.

Overall, we ended up with a clear four-step sequence, the first of which potential clients could take for free. This led neatly to the three chargeable modules.

Paul named the free lead-generation module the Employee Engagement Benchmark. Users who completed it got an overall employee-engagement score, with the option to sign up for a report giving detailed scores for the different elements that contribute to employee engagement.

Results and WEF Alignment

Comparing the project with the Website Effectiveness Framework illustrates how the framework can be used as a benchmark, to check essential points are addressed.

Cogency

The website was created after July 2019 and therefore subject to Google's mobile-first indexing policy. The site uses HTTPS, renders well on mobile devices and loads quickly.

We created two different websites, one of each of the company's main languages:

- team-andare.com – an English language site for international clients

- team-andare.nl – written in Dutch for the home market

Although the main product pages on both sites refer to the same products, the blogs carry different content, as each has articles specific to the intended readership. Having separate domains makes it much easier to serve multiple languages.

Systems and Community Engagement

Team ANDARE has excellent brand recognition in The Netherlands. Paul ter Wal, the company's founder, speaks at many English language conferences to help build the firm's international presence. To help boost the company's English language traffic, we ran an (English language based) SEO audit. We used the outcome to create regular blogposts, backlinks and internal links. Team ANDARE staff reuse some of the blogposts on social media, along with canonical tags to ensure the main site benefits from the additional exposure.

We worked with Paul to create an assessment based lead magnet called the Engagement Benchmark Tool. The website offers the tool as a starting point for potential clients who might be considering a more detailed employee engagement survey.

Users of the benchmark tool receive a guideline percentage score and can request an additional report that provides individual scores for individual categories.

Market and Client Alignment

Team ANDARE built its reputation helping Dutch companies reduce absenteeism. The ideas underpinning 'employee engagement' are newer and Team ANDARE has coupled these with work on 'company values' to create a series of programs that help companies improve their productivity.

We created the English language site first and P-CAM played an essential role in documenting the new programs. Over time, Team ANDARE staff translated core material to Dutch, and we built the Dutch language site.

For the Dutch market, the engagement-led approach to improving company performance is quite new and marks a departure from the traditional approaches to reducing absenteeism.

16.

Rainer Petek

I've had five websites built for me over the years, and I can honestly say this is the first time I've ended up with one that was really 'me'.

—Rainer Petek

**FEATURES OF WEBSITE DESIGN,
PLUS MULTIPLE-LANGUAGE SUPPORT**

Example of the value of high-quality client content and an alternative approach to website navigation

Case-Study Scope

Read this case study for an alternative view on website navigation, plus interesting design options made possible by an abundance of high-quality client-generated visual content. This is a good illustration of a visually-led design underpinned by Market Alignment work and the use of P-CAM to create new product names and descriptions.

https://rainerpetek.com and https://rainerpetek.de

Rainer Petek

Rainer Petek is a successful inspirational speaker, management consultant, and extreme mountaineer, working in German and

English. By the age of 19, he had already conquered the north face of Grandes Jorasses, one of the most difficult mountaineering challenges of the Alps. As a professional mountain guide, Rainer has led many clients on extremely difficult climbing routes in the Eastern and Western Alps. When working as a management consultant, clients love how Rainer guides them up the 'north face of business'.

The challenge of creating the website Rainer had in his mind's eye required the successful merging of mountaineering, inspirational speaking, and management consulting.

We were fortunate in that, over the years, Rainer has built up an exceptional library of very high-quality photographs and videos. This is a learning point that's really worth taking to heart: you can never have too much video or photography of your work, especially if it has a highly visual element (like mountaineering). If you run an office-based business, you might feel ill-equipped to compete with Rainer's stunning photography, but I'm willing to bet you could produce more than you initially think possible if you put your mind to it. Business awards, conferences and exhibitions, meetings with clients—these can all make great 'real-world' images of you 'doing your thing'. As they are unique and personal, they will serve you far better than stock photography. View professional photography as an investment, rather than an expense.

Looking at Rainer's site on a desktop computer, you'll see a full-width video header. Rainer was really keen on having such a feature, and as you'll recall from earlier chapters, I'm not at all in favour of video headers. Remember, they can increase website load times and make important headline text harder to read. But Rainer's the client and he really wanted a full-width video header, so we needed a solution. We started three parallel work streams: video production, homepage copy, and navigation design.

Video production

To avoid stifling the video editor's creative spirit, I gave him much more content than he needed. His task was to create a silent, lightweight (small file size), looping video that not only visually demonstrated mountaineering and inspirational speaking, but linked the two activities. I also specified that as far as possible, the overall video background should be reasonably dark, so any text the designers floated on top would render clearly and remain legible.

Clients frequently get excited with the idea of having a video header, but few have enough high-quality content to make it a practical reality. It was Rainer's huge library that made a video header viable.

Even though the video editor had quite a task, it was achievable—at least for desktop. What about mobile? I stuck to my guns and told Rainer he could have his video header on the desktop site, but we would implement a static image on the mobile site. Why? Because Google is only interested in indexing mobile versions of websites and load time is becoming a mid-ranking factor.

Homepage copy

The homepage copy—particularly the headline text over the video—needed to reinforce the connection between Rainer's mountaineering and speaking/consulting work. Rainer already had half the answer, as he already talked with his clients about 'The north face of business'. We expanded that theme, ending up with:

Meet Your Mountain Guide
for the North Face of Business

We also added this subhead:

Ready to leave base camp and achieve the summit
of your business success?

Having established the mountaineering theme on the homepage, we maintained it throughout the site. For example, we named each of Rainer's consulting interventions a type of 'expedition': the Base Camp Expedition, the High Camp Expedition, and the Summit Expedition.

Although clients don't know the exact contents of each of these 'expeditions', they intuitively see a progression from base camp to high camp and, finally, the summit. Using this simple allegory establishes an order that makes communicating the details much easier.

Navigation design

There were a couple of points that led us to think more closely about the structure of the navigation. Rainer was keen that some navigation choices be more prominent than others. The header video turned out really well and we could make overlaid text stand out.

We decided to split the navigation. The elements Rainer wanted to be prominent we placed as transparent buttons on top of the header video. We then moved all the remaining navigation to a hamburger menu. This had the added advantage of maintaining navigational similarity between the desktop and mobile sites, both of which use hamburger menus.

Website design

With the video header, navigation, and homepage copy largely decided, we could brief the designer and let him loose on the site. An important design point we had to allow for was Rainer's requirement for a dual-language site. Our solution was to build different sites: the English site would be available via RainerPetek. com, while the German site would be available at RainerPetek.de. Translating from English into other languages normally ends up with text expansion. From English to German the typical expansion is an additional 10% to 35%. The designer had to come up with a layout that would be robust enough to cope with this expansion and look good on all devices: desktop, tablet, and mobile.

Results and WEF Alignment

From a visual impact and Cogency perspective, the website looks attractive and loads quickly on all devices. Occasionally, Rainer organizes one-off events, and we support these via landing pages created on a subdomain of his main site. Rainer advertises the URL of the subdomain, for example, 'event.rainerpetek.de'.

From a Community Engagement perspective, Rainer is well known in his market, similar in that respect to Paul ter Wal in The Netherlands. We spent a long time with Rainer, talking about his business, his passion for mountaineering, and how he helps his clients with his different programs. We caught all of this in P-CAM and used it to inform our ideas for carrying the mountaineering theme through his websites. Rainer commented how challenging the process was and how deeply it caused him to think about his own business. However, it was this that led to Rainer's comment (at the start of the chapter) about the website being the first one that he felt really comfortable with. It was a great project and very enjoyable.

Coming Soon

I've already started the second book in the Website Wisdom collection. The working title is:

Websites for Non-IT Managers

This will be for people who want to get the best from their organization's website without the headache of learning geek-speak. The working subtitle, so far is:

Ditch your technobabble headache and get the website your business needs

Typical readers will be managers of non-IT departments in an SME business that's big enough to have an IT function. All departments have an increasing degree of interaction with the website.

Readers are experts in their domain (e.g. marketing, sales, HR, production, customer service) and don't necessarily understand 'website-stuff'. However, they acknowledge they need to know more about the website, as its tentacles are spreading everywhere.

This book comes to their rescue.

It'll be a quick read that will help people understand where and how websites can help the various functions within a business: sales, marketing, HR, training, customer care, etc.

If you'd like to know more about the project, I'd love to hear from you. Send me an email at: nextbook@activepresence.com.

Tell me what aspect of websites you'd like to see better explained in non-technical terms, along with your frustrations in getting the website your business deserves.

One More Thing

Just as engines need fuel to do useful work, books need reviews. I'd be most grateful if you'd leave one on the platform from where you bought your copy of *Why Your Website Doesn't Work*.

Author's Note & Acknowledgements

The answer to "How long did it take?" varies depending on perspective. I first seriously set pen to paper in October 2021 and finished the manuscript about a year later. A lot of work needs to be done to convert a manuscript into a published book (I'll come to that later), so one could say around 14 months to publication. Including P-CAM development extends the timescale, as I started working on the tool in 2019. And that was based on results from the annual Worldwide Digital Footprint survey, the first of which I ran in 2017. So, the multiple choice selection of answers is: a year, 14 months, 4 years, or 7 years. All these are academic. The proper answer—although I didn't know it at the time—is that I started work on this book when I joined the nascent IT industry over 40 years ago. Tim McGinn deserves a mention in dispatches for his encouragement and guidance during my early days at IBM. They were good days. I enjoyed them tremendously and learned a huge amount from people I'm still in touch with to this day.

The changes in information technology over my working life have been breathtaking. We have gone from an extremely limited ability to transmit data over fixed telephone lines to a universal, world-encompassing capacity to connect individual 'wireless handsets' almost anywhere on the planet.

During all this change, some approaches have remained unaltered. They've become the 'common sense' that has underpinned this new sector during its turbulent, rapid development. It's these practices and common sense that I've wanted to capture and put in your hands.

The IT industry is losing talent at an alarming rate. All the once-bright-eyed, bushy-tailed, enthusiastic youngsters who were there at the beginning are now well into their sixties, and on their way out of the door for the last time. As with all generations, the incoming one doesn't accept the 'common sense' of the older generation, no matter how many times we plead with them to take heed.

"Those were the old days," they're keen to tell us, adding, "Technology is so much more reliable now."

It's true that technology is, generally, more reliable. But people aren't. We continue to repeat the same mistakes.

Even though technology is more reliable, there's much more of it in our everyday lives, so in total there's much more that could—and does—go wrong. I want to help you get the best experience you can, for the time and money you have available.

If it takes a village to raise a child, it takes an army to produce a book—and I've been helped on my way by some real troopers. Working from the outside in, my thanks to Scott Graham for his wonderful cover. Scott's a pleasure to work with and I could have gone with any of his initial concepts. My beta readers had the final vote and Sue Evans sealed the deal with her comment, "Very you, Chris. Just the right amount of James Bond." My thanks also to my dear friend Martine Balzani, international colour designer and consultant, for her detailed advice on colours.

Moving to the inside, Brooke Carey did more heavy lifting than any editor should have to, in both raising the quality of my initial drafts and helping me raise the quality of my game as an author: thank you Brooke. Megan Sheer designed both the ebook and print formats, and did a beautiful job of making a complex topic easy to follow. My thanks to Philip Davidson for his sound studio and professional editing in creating the audiobook. My thanks to Steve Lowell for helping me organize my thoughts that led to the Website Effectiveness Framework. Thanks to Taylor Gee for supplying the brains behind the text manipulation in P-CAM. Taylor was yet another of many professionals with whom it was a pleasure to work. Creating the exemplar case study within P-CAM was a trial. I spent many hours getting nowhere before seeking help. It arrived in the guise of Melanie Votaw, who did a great job in helping me break the logjam. Katrina Nichols performed copywriting magic and produced the example product description (for Alison Tan's YFN program). Thank you both. Rob Fitzpatick runs a delightful authors' community,[25] and it's been a pleasure to work with Rob's team and the larger community during this process, sharing the trials and tribulations of getting the job done.

Pacing me on the final sprint to the finish line was Laura Maude, who provided first class proofreading. Both Brooke and Laura did sterling work in judging and guiding the mid-Atlantic house style I adopted—a mixture of traditional British and American spellings. Please let me know of any remaining errors, for they certainly belong on my desk and nowhere else.

A big vote of thanks to the clients who allowed me to use their websites as case studies. Thank you, Frank Rogers, Paul ter Wal and Rainer Petek. Thank you also to the Active Presence team, Felix, Georgina, Elmer, Marianne, and Mark. They do great work looking after our clients and the technology delivering WEA, P-CAM, etc.

I'm grateful to my mastermind buddies, Niels Brabandt and Paul ter Wal for allowing me to over-use their brains on so many occasions. I benefitted from a great crew of beta readers. My thanks to you all, in no particular order, Paul Knop, Lynda Shaw, Jason Le Masurier, Jan Kiermasz, Paul ter Wal, Heather Smith, Nigel Davis, Shirley Garrett, Angela Hurrell, Jamie Trewick, Brittany Madden, Stuart Harris, Mark Lee, Guy Clapperton, Ben Afia, Chantal Cornelius, Thorsten Jekel, Simma Lieberman, Jenny de St Georges, Bianca

25 https://writeusefulbooks.com

Kroon, Debbie Catt, Olivia James, Lindsay Adams, David Abbott, Jessica Breitenfeld, Kate Warwick, Brian Hall, Peter Gregory, Tony Altman, Paul Glynn, Nicole Wellens, and Lorne Kelton.

All projects need a Pole Star to navigate by, as does life itself. Thank you, Carol, for being mine. Dad made an appearance earlier and gets the last word:

Play to the final whistle. Don't argue with the ref.

Consolidated Nutshell Notes

Chapter 1

NUTSHELL NOTE #1

Many business owners haven't kept pace with the development of website technologies. Websites can play a more significant role than many business owners realize, but they are becoming harder to implement.

Chapter 2

NUTSHELL NOTE #2

The complexity of modern website technologies means you need a team to realize the benefits for your business. Getting the right help early on saves time and money in the long run. The tighter the initial specification, the better the end result. IT projects need specific management skills, and website owners shouldn't assume their general business management skills will suffice.

Chapter 3

NUTSHELL NOTE #3

The Website Effectiveness Framework gives business owners a structure for categorizing the common technical, marketing, and product-oriented challenges faced during website development. This helps save time and money by focusing effort where it's most needed.

Chapter 4

NUTSHELL NOTE #4

The Website Effectiveness Assessment scores the effectiveness of your website against the five tiers of the Website Effectiveness Framework. The scores help you prioritize your website-development efforts.

Chapter 5

NUTSHELL NOTE #5

Ensure all non-secure (HTTP) URLs are permanently redirected to their secure (HTTPS) equivalents. Test well to catch any dead links.

NUTSHELL NOTE #6

Delivering a good mobile experience is vital (it's the only version of your website Google indexes). Deliver all your content to all your website visitors (regardless of device).

NUTSHELL NOTE #7

Build your website on solid foundations by making sure these four areas are well configured:
- HTTPS (website security)
- Mobile experience
- Google Core Web Vitals
- Optimized Metadata

Chapter 6

NUTSHELL NOTE #8

Google Analytics is a great tool and has been around for years. Newer tools focus on the 'visitor journey' and are more useful to marketing-oriented people, such as business owners.

Chapter 7

NUTSHELL NOTE #9

Digital noise is drowning out your marketing messages. Focus on attracting the attention of high value prospects. Start by being clear on who your prospects are, what you can do for them, and where you can find them (online and offline).

Chapter 8

NUTSHELL NOTE #10

Expertise, authority, and trustworthiness (E-A-T) are important signals for Google when assessing the quality of your website—particularly so for sites dealing with services. Your money, your life (YMYL) is an additional factor that determines the standard to which Google holds your content.

Chapter 9

NUTSHELL NOTE #11

Lead magnets are important for most websites. Personalize yours to the user's individual circumstances and help them solve a pressing need. Offer some help without any requirement to sign-up.

Chapter 10

NUTSHELL NOTE #12

The Product-Client Alignment Matrix (P-CAM) helps you create better product-oriented copy for your website. It's a tool that acts as a repository and method of organization for your thoughts. It saves you time and improves the quality of your website.

Chapter 11

NUTSHELL NOTE #13

Nothing trumps knowing your perfect client better than they know themselves. Spend time working out how you could help them change their status.

Chapter 12

NUTSHELL NOTE #14

Too few businesses do a good job of focusing their products on the needs of their perfect clients. Clearly communicate your process, benefits, and guarantees, and you'll have an immediate advantage.

Chapter 13

NUTSHELL NOTE #15

Create a commanding market position by producing a permanent market change for a niche you created.

Further Reading

There are many books to help you improve your website, your business performance, and your personal performance. Here are my favourites (listed alphabetically by author's surname).

Making Your Website Work: 100 Copy & Design Tweaks for Smart Business Owners by Gill Andrews

Obviously Awesome: How to Nail Product Positioning so Customers Get It, Buy It, Love It by April Dunford

The Mom Test: How to talk to customers and learn if your business is a good idea when everyone is lying to you by Rob Fitzpatrick

Zero to Sold: How to Start, Run, and Sell a Bootstrapped Business by Arvid Kahl

Several Short Sentences About Writing by Verlyn Klinkenborg

Copywriting Strategies: A Non-Nonsense Guide to Writing Persuasive Copy for Your Business by Nicki Krawczyk

The Subtle Art of Not Giving a F*ck: A Counterintuitive Approach to Living a Good Life by Mark Manson

Essentialism: The Disciplined Pursuit of Less by Greg McKeown

Building a Brand Story: Clarify Your Message So Customers Will Listen by Donald Miller

Deep Work: Rules for Focused Success in a Distracted World by Cal Newport

Badass: Making Users Awesome by Kathy Sierra

Built to Sell: Creating a Business That Can Thrive Without You by John Warrilow

BV - #0073 - 140223 - C0 - 234/156/11 [13] - CB - 9781739230715 - Gloss Lamination